The

GENESIS
PRAYER

The

GENESIS PRAYER

Discover the Ancient Secret to
Modern Miracles

JEFFREY MEILIKEN

ST. MARTIN'S PRESS ⏗ NEW YORK

www.stmartins.com

Design by Ruth Lee Mui

Library of Congress Cataloging-in-Publication Data

Meiliken, Jeffrey.
    The Genesis prayer: discover the ancient secret to modern miracles / Jeffrey Meiliken—1st ed.
        p. cm.
    ISBN 0-312-34779-0
    EAN 978-0-312-34779-6
    1. Ana B'ko'ak. 2. Cabala—History. 3. Gematria. 4. Jewish meditations. 5. Miracles—Anecdotes. I. Title.

BM670.A66M45 2005
222'.11068—dc22   2005047703

First Edition: November 2005

10 9 8 7 6 5 4 3 2 1

CONTENTS

Part V: Enhancing the Meditation

Part VI: Breaking the Codes

ACKNOWLEDGMENTS

Endless thanks unto the Creator, blessed be He, and special thanks to my teachers HaRav and Karen Berg for their support of me and of my family, and especially for bringing this amazing gift and knowledge to us and the world. Without them, most of us may never have heard of the *Ana B'ko'ach*, let alone all its wonderful secrets. I owe them a world of gratitude.

Also special thanks to all the sages and prophets and all the *tzaddikim* of blessed memory who formed an unbroken chain preserving all these gifts and secrets from Enoch, Abraham, and Moses to R' Shimon to the Arizal, to Rav Ashlag, to my teacher's teacher, Rav Brandwein, to my teacher, HaRav, and to all of us.

My deepest and eternal thanks to Rav Brandwein for all that he's done for my family, and for enlightening me with the secrets of the Genesis Prayer.

Heartfelt thanks goes to my wife, Debbie, and my children, David and Rachel, for their love and support. And to all those at all the Kabbalah Centres and at Ascent of Safed for everything.

A hearty and limitless thanks is owed to Zion, my tireless study partner and purveyor of ancient texts, and to Nilli, my translator extraordinaire. And also to my agent, Brian DeFiore, and my editor, Sheila Curry Oakes, for all their help, guidance, and efforts.

And a special thank you and merit to Allison, Andrea, Dr. Wallace, Julio, Carmela, Gill, Gina, Graham, Marco, Martha's daughter, Miri, Mr. McGuinness, Natasha, Paul, Sammy, Scott, Tara, Zack, and all those who shared their miracle stories with us. And also to Daniel and Patty for their early support and help.

I've dedicated the book to my brother, Robert, who died long before his time, at the age of forty-two. May he rest in peace. And may the merit of all the miracles that flow from these ancient teachings and wisdom go to my children and to the furtherance and revelation of even more miracles, that we may all merit to receive them.

Introduction

THIS BOOK IS FOR ANYONE WHO WANTS A MIRACLE, HAS ever wanted to see God's work in action, or needed proof of His existence. It is for the doubters and believers alike.

If you think nothing is out there, think again. Whether you're an agnostic astrophysicist or a seminary priest, you will discover an ancient gift that works every time, no questions asked. By the time you finish this book, your perception of the universe will have changed.

If you thought God was out there but not listening, you may discover that you have been tuning into the wrong channels. It doesn't matter whether you want to call it the Light Force of God, the creative power of the Lord, or any other expression of omnipotent omniscience, because as you'll soon discover, you have the ability to tap into it. In fact, you've had the ability all along.

If you ever wondered if anyone was listening or if anyone cared, you'll soon see for yourself the benevolence that's been available to you and all of us since the dawn of time. You'll learn why the ancient sages said the Light Force *always* gives, *always* listens, and *always* answers. Find out how to get heard. Find out what you've been missing. See an infinite stream of miracles spread out before you, guiding your every step. As you rethink everything you've ever known, you'll see that life is not supposed to be difficult; man isn't supposed to suffer; fate isn't some abstraction beyond our control; and your life can indeed be wonderful.

The short prayer-meditation revealed in this book has been lying concealed within the first verse of the Bible for over three thousand years. The sages knew a secret formula that converted the Bible's first **42** letters into the universally acknowledged **42**-letter Name of God, and using modern mathematics we can reveal for ourselves how profound that formula was. At the nexus between creation and civilization, the Genesis Prayer or **42**-letter meditation was hidden from view from everyone except the ancient sages and prophets until about thirty years ago, when two-thousand-year-old writings were translated from Aramaic to Hebrew and then to English and a whole new area of study was opened up to the world. First mentioned in the *Book of Raziel,* also known as the *Book of Enoch* and sometimes as the *Book of the Generations of Adam,* it was passed on from enlightened teacher to highly selected student and used in ways we can only dream of today. This will be discussed further in Part VI, but the *Book of Enoch* was actually part of the Bible until 325 C.E. The prayer was also widely quoted, cited, or paraphrased at least one hundred times in nearly all the books of the New Testament, including Revelations.

Two thousand years earlier, by 2000 B.C.E., the Egyptians also venerated the prophet Enoch and his works. They knew him by the name Thoth, the one who brought them knowledge of astronomy, mathematics, medicine, geometry, numbers, music, botany, engineering, and the Divine Names of God. When the Greeks went to Egypt and studied their books, they brought the knowledge of Enoch/Thoth back to Greece, changing his name to Hermes, the messenger, which is another word for angel. The **42** books of Thoth, also known as the **42** Books of Instructions (an allusion to the **42**-letter Genesis Prayer), were said to reveal the secrets of the gods themselves and all that was hidden in the stars. Unfortunately, we'll never know, as these books were all destroyed in the fire that burned down the Great Library of Alexandria.

Because the *Sefer Raziel* (or the *Book of Raziel*) kept disappearing and then popping up in the hands of only a select few, including Enoch, Noah, Abraham, Shem, and King Solomon, it is considered a mystical text, yet the writings of the sages and prophets abound with references and citations from it.

As for the Genesis Prayer itself, the *Book of Raziel* spells it out exactly as we do in the enclosed meditations: **42** specific words that describe God's greatness and our humbleness, associated with **42** specific letters arrayed in 7 lines and split into 2 triplets per line. The *Book of Raziel* describes the Prayer as follows:

> This is a holy Name. It is revealed by the combination going forth from the beginning scriptures in the Torah. From the *Bet of Beresheit* [the first letter in the Bible] until the *Bet of Bohu* [the **42**nd letter]. Knowledge of the wisdom of the Torah completes the Names of God, blessed are they. The rows of marks [letters] reveal the knowledge and wisdom is revealed.

The Genesis Prayer was expounded upon in the *Torot Hakuna* two thousand years ago and then again in the *Zohar*, nineteen hundred years ago, and then here and there in whispered writings, all but disappearing until about five hundred years ago when it reappeared in the ultracomplex and brilliantly coded writings of Isaac Luria (commonly referred to as the *Arizal*), where we were given innumerable clues as to its power. It was the *Arizal* who advised us about the encrypted mathematics in the Prayer and the Torah (Pentateuch) and about what these connected to and what they revealed, explaining which Names of God were associated with which verses and which gates these opened for us, figuratively and literally—in other words, what we could get out of them and how to use them.

Sages throughout the centuries continued to use the prayer, albeit discreetly, and every once in a while they'd mention it in their writings, as Maimonides did in the 1100s. He concluded that the **42** letters formed several words, each expressing a definitive idea or fundamental attribute of the Supreme Being, and all together providing the true definition of the divine essence, which is another reason why the sages all referred to the Genesis Prayer as the **42-letter Name of God**; *it's that important!* Much earlier than Maimonides, the *Talmud* states:

> The forty-two lettered Name is entrusted only to him who is pious, meek, middle-aged, free from bad temper, sober, and not insistent on his rights. And he who knows it, is heedful thereof, and observes it in purity, is beloved above and popular below, feared by man, and inherits two worlds, this world and the future world.

While the writings in the *Talmud* are timeless, the *Zohar* adds that it would be our generation, the generation of knowledge, that would receive this knowledge and insights openly. The sages explain that each generation is different from its predecessor in its ability to process and utilize the various spiritual tools, so while the preferred level of purity stated above would be beneficial to all, it's no longer a requirement.

The fifteenth-century Byzantine text the *Sefer Ha-Peliyah* describes how the Archangel Metatron himself dictated the wisdom of the Genesis Prayer to R' Hakana, the author of the *Torot Hakuna,* but where he got his information from we can only speculate. We do know that great sages and scholars like Rabbeinu Tam, Rabbi Abraham Abulafia, and Moshe Cordevero, from the eleventh, thirteenth, and sixteenth centuries respectively, wrote about it openly; nevertheless, they reserved most of the more powerful meditations for their select pupils. And so it's been for thousands of years, from patriarch to prophet to sage, the wisdom and knowledge of the Genesis Prayer have been secretly passed down and passed around. About thirty years ago that all changed.

My teacher, Rav Berg, who learned of the Genesis Prayer from his teacher, Rav Brandwein, and from his teacher in turn, decided it was time for man—all men, women, and children—to benefit from the hidden blessings of the Genesis Prayer, the most powerful prayer of all time. The second-century *Zohar,* which spoke extensively about the Genesis Prayer, spoke about our generation eighteen hundred years hence as being the "generation of knowledge," and judging by our computer/Internet/information revolution, who's to argue? But it also said that this was the generation in which all the ancient secrets were to be revealed. First among those secrets is the Genesis Prayer. At first, Rav Berg introduced it to only a select few, but as time went on and he realized how many benefits his students were deriving from it, he wished to expand his teachings. That's when he moved from Jerusalem to the United States and brought with him some of the greatest wisdom and deepest secrets man has ever known. He has counseled kings and presidents and has helped millions of people. Today more than five hundred thousand people have learned some of the secrets of the Genesis Prayer and brought miracles into their lives. It's with the utmost respect for my teacher, his teacher, Rav Brandwein, and all the sages, prophets, and patriarchs of blessed memory before them that we reveal the rest of the secrets known to us of the Genesis Prayer, and open once and for all the floodgates of knowledge. It's with Rav Berg's permission and blessing that we can all now partake of this ancient wisdom through which wars have been won, hearts have been mended, women have conceived, and untold lives have been saved.

The Genesis Prayer is built up of three essential components. The first is the **42** letters themselves, the scaffolding upon which the meditations hang. They are akin to the skeleton of a skyscraper, while the meditations are the windows, walls, wiring, and everything else that makes the skyscraper inhabitable. Without the meditations, the **42** letters are all but useless to us. *This* is the component that has been concealed from us for so long. The third component we spoke of is more abstract. It's the breath that God blew into Adam. It's the unspoken essence that makes a painting beautiful or a sunset inspire awe. It's the essence that our consciousness taps into when we do the prayer. It's what gets activated when we do the meditations, and it's what causes those meditations to bring miracles into our lives.

While the meditations that activate the Genesis Prayer have been hidden for millennia, the Prayer itself has been an integral part of the Friday night services seemingly forever. Generations have recited it, never knowing about the power that lay within it, only that it was there in their prayer books and thus some sage or prophet must have said it's beneficial. It was only about forty years ago that the books of the sixteenth-century Arizal and the eighteenth-century Rashash were openly decrypted and we learned that the Genesis Prayer is so powerful that several of the most important prayers in the Jewish services are designed to connect to its energy: the first blessing in the *Amidah,* or silent meditation said three times a day, has, not coincidentally, **42** words; likewise, the first paragraph of the best-known Jewish prayer, the *Schma,* has **42** words; and the first verse of the concluding prayer, *Aleinu Le Shabe'ach,* has the same numerical value as the Genesis Prayer's first verse. While these prayers are found only in Jewish services, versions of the Genesis Prayer meditations, which predated the formation of all religions, have found their way into the teachings of all major faiths.

It was because of this profound and illuminating work of the Arizal and his student R. Chaim Vittal that our consciousness was awoken and we knew to look deeper. Rav Brandwein and his teacher searched back another thirteen hundred years further in time and turned their attention to the nineteen-hundred-year-old *Zohar.* Today, while it's still very cryptic, it has been translated into English. When they first began studying it, the *Zohar* was very dense nonannotated Aramaic. Still, numerous references to the Genesis Prayer and its power emerged, including a few clues as to what line connected to what energy. Extraordinary power was at their fingertips; they could feel it. During the 1960s, when they were conducting their research, *everyone* could feel the energy shift. It has taken years and years of research, investigation, decryption, and dumb luck to bring to light the secrets of the sages, and many of the deepest secrets about the Genesis Prayer still remain cloaked beneath the surface, but the more people who recite the prayer and do its meditations, the easier it will be for additional secrets to find their way to our collective consciousness.

There are many scholars who insist that the Pentateuch (the Torah, or Five Books of Moses) was written by several different sources in several distinct voices. This, of course, ignored what the Bible tells us about the seven voices of God and His thirteen attributes, and at one time I counted myself among those scholars. Indeed, I once thought that anything to do with the Bible or with quotes attributed to God couldn't have been anything more than wishful thinking, but then how could I explain how pi, phi, and alpha—three constants arguably created at the dawn of time—were intimately encoded into the Bible's first verse? I couldn't. The simplest of equations directly derived from this verse yielded all three primordial constants, to up to thirteen decimal places, no less. Nor could I explain how the number of character elements—the sum of the letters, words, and verses—in the Pentateuch wound up being exactly 5^8. I couldn't—no one can. When I discovered that the Pentateuch has exactly $5 \times 5 \times 5 \times 5 \times 5 \times 5 \times 5 \times 5$ words, letters, and verses, it was a watershed moment in my life. Of course it had to be a high multiple of 5, like 5^8, the sages always drew parallels to the 5 Books of Moses, the 5 levels of our souls, the 5 worlds or levels of consciousness, the 5 core dimensions, the 5 times the word "light" appears in the first day of creation, and even our 5 senses. And as the Arizal explains, there are 8 distinct brushstrokes that make up the 5 specific parts of the Tetragrammaton (יהוה), and the number 8 represents the *brit,* God's Covenant, so what can be more perfect than the Torah being represented by a single number 5^8? It was mind-boggling that a document with over three hundred thousand characters, nearly twice the length of this book, and written entirely by hand on cured animal skins could have worked out so extraordinarily precisely. It was obviously no accident. To have been created by man to that precision without the aid of computers, calculators, or word-processing and counting software would have added lifetimes to the actual writing. A coincidence? Hardly. It is as if you were told to mark off some space on a beach, and afterward you were told there had to be exactly 390,625 grains of sand in it, and after a thorough counting you wound up with exactly 390,625 grains of sand. Could it happen? Sure, but what would be the odds?

That's why I knew I had to look deeper into the Pentateuch (Torah) and look to the ancient books of the many sages who dissected it. The deeper I looked, the more beautiful things got. What I found eventually led to the writing of this book. It was only the beginning. It was no accident. And there were no other explanations. I tried them all. Then I tried the Genesis Prayer.

I was convinced.

The deeper I dug, the more convinced I became. While using the writings of the sages to guide me, and my computer to do the computational legwork, it became apparent that something far greater was going on than even my teacher had apprised me, which isn't surprising because he only reveals the secrets that he feels someone is ready to hear. But you can discover that for yourself; it should leap off these pages as it did for me.

If any prayer has ever moved you, imagine how much more you'll be moved by the very first one in the Bible. If you've ever been moved by a meditation, imagine how much more you'll be by the one used by the prophets and sages to elevate their souls. And if you've ever experienced miracles, imagine how much easier life will be when you recite the prayer that *promises* to bring them to you on command, as it has to countless others.

They say, everything in its time. This is our time. Yes, all the secret codes and unfathomable scientific evidence lying in the Bible out of plain sight were known to the ancient sages, and yes, they were always there, but only our generation has the computational tools and the generalized scientific wherewithal to recognize them for what they are and what they prove.

There's no doubt about it: we were the ones meant to rediscover the Genesis Prayer. Of all the generations, it's our generation, the one of the least faith, who need it the most. We're the ones who demand proof. Now we have it. We're the ones who demand instant gratification. Now we can get it. Unwittingly perhaps, we demanded the Genesis Prayer. Now we've got it.

There's an ancient maxim: As below, above. Contrary to the times of the sages, our complex lives and society have so polluted and clouded the atmosphere that there's only one way to get our voices heard through the din of the corrupting static: to go back to the beginning, to the place of the Genesis Prayer, to the Bible's very first verse, to man's first gift. Regardless of our natural skepticism, in less than five minutes we'll see the earth shift around us, get our miracles, and prove it for ourselves without further prompting.

Einstein once said, "God doesn't play dice with the universe"; come find out how you can stack the odds.

PART I

MY JOURNEY

1

I Discover the Power of the Genesis Prayer

MY STORY WITH THE GENESIS PRAYER, OR *ANA B'KO'ACK* (pronounced *Anna BeKo-ak*), began five years ago when I started studying the pre-Islamic, pre-Christian, pre-Jewish, pre-Buddhist writings of Abraham and the ancient sages, the universal foundations on which all religions were originally based. I'd studied Christianity, Buddhism, both North American and South American shamanism, and even aboriginal dreamtime, wherever my research and personal journey took me, but I never settled long in any one place until my teacher, Rav Berg, revealed the true secrets behind what I was seeking. Yes, I had an advantage over most of those who'd rediscovered these teachings after thirty-four hundred years of near-total concealment. I was already certain that God existed; I was only looking for ways to *prove* it to others. I knew in my heart that the precision and advanced mathematical concepts I'd found while examining other ancient structures would hold true for the Bible as well, that the mathematical evidence pointing to an origin beyond our capabilities would be there. Because I already had strong clues to go on, I was certain I could find this evidence, which was important to me because I wanted to share this certainty. When we don't know something for sure, doubts creep in, but if I could give people something concrete, they, too, could share in the benefits of certainty, especially in these most uncertain times.

Also, thanks to my varied journey, I'd already been to the spiritual places and experienced the cognitive transitions described in the ancient books my teacher suggested: books like the *Sefer Yetzirah* (the *Book of Formation*), written by Abraham, the Patriarch, thirty-eight hundred years ago; the *Bahir,* written over two thousand years ago; and the *Zohar* (the *Book of Splendor*), written nearly nineteen hundred years ago by one of the greatest sages of all time, R. Shimon Bar Yochai. Nevertheless, after five months of studying the writings of the sages, my pursuits were all intellectual, all about the knowledge, until I took a trip to Israel, my first, to visit some of those power vortices and ancient sites spoken about in the books for myself.

Rav Berg told me that the best way to tell the importance of a prayer or meditation is by how little attention is lavished on it by traditionalists, and by that reckoning the Genesis Prayer, being one of the most overlooked prayers in Judeo-Christian practice, ranks as extremely powerful. I was to find out just how potent that fateful afternoon. My studies had taken me in so many different directions that in my time of greatest need I, too, almost overlooked the Genesis Prayer.

It was late in the afternoon and I had a couple of hours to kill before meeting up with one of my teacher's senior students in central Jerusalem. He suggested Rachel's Tomb, the Matriarch's Tomb in Bethlehem, one of those earthly power spots where one can make powerful spiritual connections. He said it was an easy drive, practically a straight line, and right off the highway. I never made it there.

The highway was closed by the military, the traffic was detoured, and no one spoke enough English to explain why. Some of the many lessons I learned on that trip was that I couldn't do everything on my own and that I couldn't be so blindly stubborn and determined, especially since I didn't speak Hebrew, none whatsoever. But life's a process and I was thick in the middle of it. Undaunted by the odds, I followed the traffic and made my way through a tunnel and onto a parallel highway, exiting where I estimated the back roads would lead me up and over a hill to Rachel's Tomb. That was my first mistake. I had no idea that would take me through the heart of Palestine.

Talking my way past the Palestinian policeman with the sadistic gleam in his eye was my next mistake. Two blocks from the highway there was a makeshift barricade and I, along with all the other cars with Israeli plates, had been stopped and ordered to turn around. With my inflated ego still intact, I refused, invoking my Americanism as my right to pass. Forget the fact that I was wearing a yarmulke (skullcap), which I'd only decided to wear since my arrival a few days earlier, and that I hadn't had the foresight to remove it. Insistent as I was, he told me to pull over; he was taking me to jail. Only the kindheartedness or levelheadedness of another guard saved me that time. He waved me through when the other turned his back. Not turning and running was my next mistake.

Shaken, yet still determined to climb the hill, I came to a dead halt as the traffic came to a standstill not halfway up. We all crawled the rest of the way, my plates and conspicuous yarmulke sticking out like a sore thumb and causing many a caustic glance. Before long, we made it to the top of the hill and the main part of town, and I'd even managed to hide the skullcap beneath my seat. But I still had no idea what was going on, where I was going, or even where I was. Through repeated attempts and broken English, though, I realized I wasn't going to get to Rachel's Tomb, and getting out alive should be my first priority.

There were only three main exits to town, one of which was back down the hill into the hands of the guard who wanted to jail me before I outwitted him. I could only imagine what he wanted to do to me now. He wasn't going to get the chance. Both of the other thoroughfares were sealed off tight by ill-tempered guards with machine guns, and the side streets around them were choked off by traffic, some as desperate as me, but at least they understood what was going on. I was pretty much left with my imagination.

After being turned away from both gates, I peeled off the ever-lengthening traffic line and made my way onto a back road. The years I'd spent in South America numbed me from fear of gravel roads that turned into ever-narrower dirt roads, then steep paths—I knew one of them had to lead back down the hill. Yet they didn't. They all led toward more hills and deeper into Palestine, forcing me to retreat, dangerously doubling back over steep precipices. Like cats in the night, distinctly malevolent stares pierced the deepening shadows, eyeing the plates on my car. It wasn't the roads that frightened me; it was the darkness. Dusk had descended swiftly, and on dirt roads, there are no streetlights.

I made it back to town as nightfall officially descended, and after being turned away by an angry guard, I tried my luck on one of those interminable traffic lines to nowhere. Someone with a British accent informed me that the Israelis had ordered the town sealed off for security reasons. I didn't know it at the time, but the *intifada* was only weeks away. I tried the roadblock with the angry guard yet again—what else could I do—but he snarled back, menacing me with the muzzle of his submachine gun, indicating that he'd already told me to turn around once.

A woman with a reliable voice told me that the only way out was down the other side of the hill, but that meant getting past the guard with the angry gun, not to mention his well-armed buddies, a paramilitary force with more in common with the PLO than the NYPD.

I called Moshe, for whom I was already an hour late, and he asked if I'd tried the *Ana B'ko'ack* yet. I'd forgotten all about it, and was pretty nervous by then, so he talked me through it, instructing me to relax and meditate on the *Ana B'ko'ack* yet again when I'd calmed down. I told him I'd check back in half an hour and then repeated the meditation, this time recalling the words of our teacher: Everything is an illusion, and the Genesis Prayer is our tool to see past it. As I said to myself, "It's all an illusion," I approached the guard for the third time, and told him I was going down the hill.

He waved me through. With the makeshift gate swinging shut

behind me, I sped around the corner and down the hill. Miraculously, I found the original closed highway, and was whisked back into Israeli territory. Whether the Genesis Prayer saved my life that night, or only saved me from a frightful couple of perplexing days in an increasingly antagonistic Palestine with my Israeli rental car, I'll never know, but it did clue me in to the enormous power hidden within the short, seven-line, **42**-word meditation called the *Ana B'ko'ack,* or Genesis Prayer.

I saw the miracle firsthand, saw it in the face of the guard who only minutes earlier was willing to shoot me just for being a nuisance, but suddenly didn't recognize me or my American face. Something had shifted in the universe. From other spiritual practices I knew it as a paradigm shift, something only master practitioners could do, but I was a novice, a rank novice, reciting the prayer only for the first time under real-life conditions. Could it really have been that easy? I was thankful for the experience and for the knowledge that I now had a new tool to help me get through life, but I'd gained even more. A gateway had opened for me; the parallel universe I'd shifted into would never be the same. My journey had just begun.

PART II

MIRACLES AND
WONDERS

2

Seeing Past the Illusions

THE GENESIS PRAYER, OVERLOOKED BY TRADITIONALISTS and admittedly by myself, was formerly used by the ancient sages to elevate their consciousness through seven levels of understanding to a place where all the illusions would fade, laying bare the underlying structure of the universe. Because the shells of darkness we've built around ourselves are much thicker today, the best we can do is use the Genesis Prayer to get miracles, which is quite an understatement, seeing as many of us go through our whole life wishing for a miracle.

Unlike us, the sages could see how the system worked. We can dissect the Genesis Prayer and examine its hidden codes, but we can't really grasp what they connect to, what their corresponding energies and sources mean. Fortunately, we don't have to understand how it works in order to receive the miracles. However, it is important to consider what illusions stand in the way of our understanding.

The first illusion is that our destiny is set in stone. Through my research into many ancient monuments and documents, I have discovered that the only things immutable in our universe are the mathematical constants created at the dawn of time. Why this is important will be explained later when we discuss where exactly the

Genesis Prayer came from. For now, we'll stick to the illusions, like the one I had in Palestine that "no" meant "no," that the situation I was in was a curse and not the blessing it turned out to be. Had I not had that harrowing experience, I never would have written this book. Once I realized that everything I was going through was a process to teach me a lesson—not a punishment, but a lesson in the functioning of life and my place in it—the illusion vanished and the gate swung open.

MAKING CHOICES

Life is full of choices. We literally make thousands of them every day, but because our scope of vision is so limited we frequently make the wrong ones, even if they seem right at the time. There are billions of parallel paths we can take, each one a slight variation of the previous one, and while one of them leads us to our maximum true fulfillment and spiritual accomplishment, one also leads us to the worst possible place. We are lost somewhere between the two extremes, with very little information to go on and no road map to guide us.

Each step we take, or choice we make, determines which path we'll move along, and because this process is entirely controlled by our consciousness it can appear to be simultaneously a blessing and a curse: a blessing because we have complete free will, a curse because we have very little control over our consciousness. The sages tell us that the essence of the entire Bible is contained in the spiritual verse from Leviticus, "And you shall love your neighbor as yourself," so try and keep your thoughts pure and filled with unconditional love and an unconditional desire to share what that verse embodies. How long could you hold it? Most of us can't even keep our minds from wandering for more than a few seconds, let alone direct and hold our thoughts in such a pure state. That's why we need help. That's why we need the Genesis Prayer.

The Genesis Prayer takes the guesswork out of the equation. Just as I experienced, and as tens of thousands of others have, too, the Genesis Prayer automatically shifts us to a better universe, one step closer, maybe a giant step, to that state of fulfillment.

SEEING THE BIG PICTURE

It's easy to understand why we make the wrong choices. After all, we see so little of the big picture. Take a step back and take a look at our convoluted busy lives and the constant barrage of information that's thrown at us daily, unprecedented in the history of the world: newspapers and twenty-four-hour news reports from every corner of the globe; relentless e-mails and faxes; phone calls wherever we are, crossing the street or on the toilet; Internet searches; junk mail; advertising wherever we look, from the shopping cart itself to the roofs and backseats of our taxicabs, not to mention TV, radio, and our computers; add to that the copious amount of gossip to which we voluntarily and sometimes gleefully subject ourselves from the office water coolers to electronic missives to the magazines piled high at every turn; and then there's the actual messages we do need, like how our spouses and children feel, what they did during the day, and what we can do to help our friends and society. Is it any wonder we are overloaded and can't see beyond our noses?

It's easy to see why people in Biblical times with so fewer distractions and so much more time to reflect were so much more spiritual, and yet, even then, only a few of them could see the consequences of their actions. With all that blinds us today, can we possibly see what effect our words will have on a friend twenty years from now, or what the consequences will be on our health fifty years down the road from eating our dinner while angry at a boss who slighted us? No. Most of us would be unaware of the consequences of our actions on our society and environment if they occurred next week, let alone sometime off in the future. We've all heard about the chaos theory allusion in which a butterfly beating its wings in China eventually causes a fierce thunderstorm over Texas; could the butterfly have known about the devastation he caused? No, because he can't see the big picture any more than we can.

A chess grandmaster can see dozens of moves down the road when he's totally focused on the game, but of course that's to the exclusion of all else. We're told the sages had this vision; they could look at you and see your entire life. We can't, but the Genesis Prayer can; it can tap into the universe, see the future, and choose the right path for us. Given our limited vision, we can't possibly make the best choices, but the Genesis Prayer changes all that; with almost no effort on our part, it expands our horizons, our external and internal vision, and sets us on a better parallel path. That's why it's called a gift. It makes the choices for us, the right choices, not the ones we'd make. We'll explore how later, but first let's examine some real-life examples from people who've used the Genesis Prayer to change their lives and the universe around them.

THE ULTIMATE MIRACLE

The Genesis Prayer, like most meditations, can be recited in a few seconds if necessary, or in five minutes if its full effect is desired, or as I've demonstrated in numerous lectures, it can be done in more than a half hour and is especially powerful when done together with a large group looking to improve the world.

My wife and I have found that the Genesis Prayer works best when a situation looks hopeless, and that it works both quicker and stronger when we do it together. I'll get to the story of the first time we did it in tandem in a moment—the whole universe seemed to bend for us, like something out of *The Twilight Zone*—but first I'd like to tell you about Andrea and the ultimate miracle.

Having dedicated herself to her career, Andrea married relatively late in life, and by the time she decided to have children the odds were stacked against her. According to her doctor at one of the country's top reproductive clinics, even with all the help that modern medicine can offer, the odds of a healthy forty-five-year-old woman going full term and giving birth to a healthy baby were less than 3 percent. Undaunted and desperate, as most couples are in their situation, Andrea and her husband pressed forward and followed all their doctor's exhausting procedures, month after month. The costs and disappointments grew. There was a heart-breaking false pregnancy reading one month, and the couple had to go through an emotionally wrenching weekend thinking she might actually be pregnant. Time wasn't on their side.

At forty-six, her odds shrank to 1 percent—that's one in a hundred assisted attempts. Each cycle of Inter Uterine Insemination (IUI) involved coming into Manhattan early every morning for nearly two weeks to have blood drawn, take hormone injections in her belly, and have ultrasounds, then wait two weeks to get the results through yet another blood test. Each time, her husband was by her side. They were not alone; Andrea estimates there were a hundred women in the waiting room every morning by 8:00 A.M., even on Sundays.

Still, after the emotional roller coaster of seven cycles of hope and disappointment, thirteen months with the down cycles and missed opportunities due to traveling and holidays, their doctor was cautiously optimistic that if they'd try the more invasive in vitro fertilization (IVF) method, maybe two or three cycles at more than $15,000 each should do the trick, but of course, there were no guarantees. The clock was ticking down. Their debts were climbing up.

They'd hoped all along to conceive as naturally as possible, and Andrea begged her doctor for the chance to do one more of the simpler IUI cycles, to which he acquiesced reluctantly. In the meantime a friend of hers recommended the Genesis Prayer. Her friend advised that she should meditate with it before the insemination procedure.

Unbeknownst to Andrea, her husband had taken an advanced meditation course and had just begun doing the Genesis Prayer, with special emphasis on its optional healing properties.

Their first surprise came when they encountered the commotion at the lab; neither the nurses nor the doctors could believe their eyes. Each month her husband had to give a sperm specimen for the insemination, which they tried to do as naturally as possible, further complicating the process, and each time he had had decent results considering his age, but not great ones, particularly regarding the motility (or mobility) of the sperm. This time his test results improved 50 percent. This level of improvement had never happened before, to anyone. The doctors were astonished and wanted to know what he'd done, but were skeptical when he said the only thing he'd done different was the meditation. His sperm's motility rate doubled, the quality of the sperm improved 40 percent, and the concentration of sperm nearly doubled. These results were unheard of!

During the IUI cycle process, the lab technicians screen, concentrate, and purify the sperm samples to improve the odds. Andrea's husband improved the odds himself, and with more viable sperm to work with the couple had their best chance yet. Andrea increased their chances when she repeated the Genesis Prayer again.

The next surprise came two weeks later, when the doctor himself called to tell Andrea she was pregnant. *Bli ayn hara,* she had a healthy baby boy.

Bli ayn hara (pronounced *blee eye-in ha-ra*) is a coded phrase that means "against evil eye"; it's a protective shield used by the sages so that neither our own egos nor other people's jealousy can attach to the words we speak. In that way we keep away the judgment that can accrue and spoil the good intentions we had in relating our tale. We'll be using this phrase from time to time to protect the integrity of those people who have graciously supplied us with their Genesis Prayer miracle stories.

What else can we say? The miracle of birth is the greatest miracle of all. But if you think about it, why shouldn't the Genesis Prayer help with conception and childbirth? After all, it connects directly with creation and the seed level of the universe, the fundamental formation of all existence. Neither time nor money can do what the Genesis Prayer can. Can you buy having your life saved? Buy giving birth to your child? Blessings aren't bought; they're earned. But that also means they have to be heard. And that takes hard work and tears. There's an ancient saying that God always hears the tears, but tears mean pain, which is what we can avoid with some forethought and the Genesis Prayer.

3

Bending the Laws of Physics

Aɴᴅʀᴇᴀ ᴀɴᴅ ʜᴇʀ ʜᴜsʙᴀɴᴅ ᴡᴇʀᴇ ʙᴏᴛʜ ᴅᴏɪɴɢ ᴛʜᴇ Genesis Prayer independently of one another, and their combined efforts brought about the greatest miracle of all. Now here's the story I promised you about when my wife and I first did the Prayer together. About two years ago, we'd gotten a late start returning from our Passover holiday in San Diego and we needed to get to LAX in Los Angeles to catch our flight back to New York. We were traveling north with our baby on Interstate 5 when traffic thickened and then stalled completely, and the tight two-hour window we'd allotted ourselves suddenly looked not only foolish, but ridiculous. At the pace we were going and had been going for more than forty-five minutes, it would take us another four hours to reach the 405 highway and then the airport. It all looked lost and we began making contingency plans about who we could stay overnight with in L.A. and where to pick up more diapers, more baby food, and so on.

Yes, we could miss our flight, but the next available one meant waiting around all day and taking the redeye, a thought neither of us relished, as we were tired and I had an important meeting first thing in the morning. Moreover, if my son didn't sleep on the overnight flight, we'd all be miserable.

No, it would not have been the end of the world, and no, we weren't bringing a new life into the world, but why go through all that inconvenience if it could be avoided? Life's not supposed to be that hard. That's what my teacher kept telling me, at any rate. So in the thick of the traffic I took us through the full version of the Genesis Prayer, with my wife and me reciting each line out loud together, and by the time we'd finished reciting the prayer and whispering the last line, sealing and manifesting the connection that we'd just made, the traffic had not only let up, but had disappeared entirely. In seconds the traffic was doing 80 mph and we raced along at that pace onto the 405 and all the way to the exit ramp by the airport. We looked at each other and knew.

That was the first time we'd tried the Genesis Prayer on traffic, the first of many, and we were, to say the least, amazed. Now we almost take it for granted, but back then we were excited and very relieved. Then, as if to cement our relationship with and certainty in the Genesis Prayer, the universe closed ranks again as we drove up the exit ramp. Just as we rounded the bend, the traffic on the highway stopped cold and became an endless snaking parking lot stretching all the way to downtown L.A. We breezed through to the airport, and—*bli ayn hara*—made our flight with plenty of time. It was as if a time tunnel or, as physicists call them, a quantum wormhole, had opened up in the universe and whisked us through it. It wasn't a lifesaving miracle, but it was one nonetheless.

YOU CAN'T ALWAYS GET WHAT YOU WANT; YOU GET WHAT YOU NEED

The next tale we'll examine is one of the ultimate of mercy. It's also about the universe giving us exactly what we need whether we know it or not, whether we see it right away or not at all. When we explain where the Genesis Prayer comes from and what it physically and metaphysically connects to, even the most diehard right-brain skeptic will share the faith and be able to appreciate not only the complexity of the universe laid bare, but its simplicity as well. Since the first revelations about the Genesis Prayer were uncloaked thirty years ago, hundreds of thousands have been able to take advantage of it. My teacher's teacher's teacher, Rav Ashlag, was a prolific writer, translating and deciphering many of the esoteric and cryptic Aramaic texts into the language of today. Still, those texts were beyond the comprehension of most men, and it took another two generations of teachers and pupils to filter them down to a level where we could grasp their principles. Over the past thirty years, more and more of the ancient wisdom and knowledge about the workings of the Genesis Prayer has come to light. Now, with the latest revelations, this knowledge and powerful meditation will be available to everyone.

Before we delve into this next and most incredible miracle story, as told to me and dozens of other witnesses not twenty-four hours after it occurred, I'd like to reiterate that the strength of the Genesis Prayer is in your consciousness and not in how long you took to recite it—of course, a longer meditation with the same consciousness is better, time permitting. It all depends on where your head is at and what your needs are, your true needs, which often, as you'll see in Allison's, and also in Scott's and Carmela's, stories, are what we least expect.

That said, Allison, an attractive young newlywed, left for work at her prestigious insurance company without doing the complete Genesis Prayer. Since she was accustomed to doing it every morning, it gnawed at her all the way to the subway that she needed to do it right. Even though she had the prayer memorized, she wanted to glance at the accompanying names of the daily angels for protection, and she'd left them behind at her apartment. These angelic energy forces (stated in Appendix Four) are tuned into the particular energy cycle of a given day of the week. They can also be thought of as quantum carrier messengers, or the fine-tune dial on a two-way radio.

Allison was already a little late, and returning home would make her later yet, which wasn't good, as she was up against a deadline. Nevertheless, she went home, and was quite late by the time she caught the downtown subway.

Setting in, she inconspicuously did the rest of the Genesis Prayer and, feeling anxious about being late, heard over the garbled intercom that the train would be detoured and pass her stop. No one on the subway car was happy; they were all probably late for work. Still, what could she do? She let go, and decided what will be will be; she'd made her choice and would have to live with it. Live she did. Coming out of the subway platform, she watched in horror as her office high up in the World Trade Center came crashing to the ground.

Tired, dust-laden, and emotionally exhausted, she made her way back home on foot. Collapsing in tears in her husband's arms, they gave thanks and credit where it was due. It was a horrible time for all of us, and Allison still shakes when she thinks of the people in her building and what might have been. A matter of minutes prevented Allison from being in her office that day. Often that's all we can hope for, buying ourselves a few more minutes, or hoping that someone makes the right call when push comes to shove. It's in times like those that the Genesis Prayer works best.

We all went through judgment that day, some much more than others, but thank God, Allison's was muted with mercy. *(Bli ayn hara.)*

For her part, Allison's close encounter was a huge awakening, and she became an even more sharing and giving person than she was already. Allison had already set herself on a spiritual path and was already getting in tune with the workings and energies of the universe. She was already making the connections that ultimately saved her life. *(Bli ayn hara.)*

With a little help and the right consciousness, we can avoid the chaos and stress that permeate our society. Consciousness alone can't do it, though. Many people have good intentions, but what they're missing is a way of activating them. It's not enough to sit on a mountain and meditate on world peace; we have to take physical action as well. The Genesis Prayer acts as a nexus between the physical and spiritual worlds. Treading both worlds at once, the reciting of the Genesis Prayer serves as doing a physical action, the right physical action to manifest the spiritual connection and create the right miracles. We can always do more, though, and spirituality is all about going the extra mile, so by doing true physical actions that benefit society and put the needs of others first, we strengthen our consciousness and thus make the Genesis Prayer work even harder for us, bringing even greater miracles into our lives, like the one Andrea experienced in having a baby.

My teacher, Rav Berg, often notes that the real miracles are the unseen ones, the ones that get you home safely every day without incident. Getting through a car accident dazed but unscathed isn't nearly as big a miracle as *not* getting into one in the first place, but because we can't control the negativity that builds up in the world around us, and can't know karmically what we need to go through in order to wake something inside us, we need a little extra help. As we can see from Allison's amazing story, it's best to do the Genesis Prayer first thing in the morning, because you never know what the day will bring. Think of the Genesis Prayer as an insurance policy that will cloak you in protection throughout your day.

Every day the news is filled with tragedies that make our lives feel so fragile and subject to fate. The real tragedy is that it doesn't have to be that way. Accidents do happen, and there is always a cause and effect beyond our vision and comprehension, but shortly we'll catch a small glimpse into that beyond and gain a little comprehension of what it's all about, but most important, we'll get an understanding of how to avoid these cosmic pitfalls. It is actually quite simple.

JUDGMENT AND MERCY

Carmela had a back problem, and usually the first sign that it was flaring up was difficulty swallowing. So when she gagged on water, she understood what was happening and instead of passing out, she did a rapid-fire silent *Ana B'ko'ack*. It probably took her all of ten seconds, and because she was used to doing the Genesis Prayer regularly, the first line is really all she needed; it's the one to use in emergencies, like dialing 911 to heaven. Nevertheless, the meditation worked and she gulped down the water. We could write this off to the calming effect of meditation, but it is only the precursor to the real tale.

Because she knew her back attack was imminent she flagged a cab and headed to her doctor. Along the way, Carmela repeated the Genesis Prayer over and over again. She didn't know why, but she couldn't help herself. She assumed it was something she needed to do for her back and didn't resist the strange urge.

A little later that day she learned that her daughter had been in a serious car accident at the same time Carmela was relentlessly reciting the Genesis Prayer in the back of the cab. Her daughter was fine, unscathed actually *(Bli ayn hara),* but the car was totaled.

Here was a situation where the prime beneficiary was someone who wasn't aware that the Genesis Prayer was being recited. In fact, it was being recited by someone (Carmela) who wasn't even asking for anything in particular, least of all for the beneficiary (her daughter), except, of course, in the general sense that Carmela's daughter was within her immediate sphere of influence and was therefore probably always in her mind. How did the Prayer's protection and aid reach out for Carmela's daughter?

Carmela had asked for help, and the universe replied by giving her just what she needed, whether or not she was aware of her need at the time. Carmela had no way of seeing the big picture, but she didn't have to; the universe did it for her and took care of it for her. When you do the Genesis Prayer you're connected to the greater universe, to everyone, everything, and every aspect of that universe at once—what physicists call quantum technology. Doing the Genesis Prayer is all it takes, that, and a positive consciousness. The beneficent light of the universe always wants to give to us, but first we have to be open to receive it. The Genesis Prayer acts as a signal flare, telling the universe we're open, we're here, and we're ready and willing to accept its help.

You might be skeptical at this point, thinking this is just a coincidence. I might be, too, if I hadn't seen too many coincidences for any of them to be random occurrences. One similar experience comes to mind. It happened to Scott as I was writing this book. I was explaining to him the magic and power in the Genesis Prayer's first line. I told him the story of a couple in Toronto whom it saved from an attacker, and he read the line aloud as I was transliterating it into this book. Nothing happened at that moment, at least that we were aware of at the time, and there was no need for anything to happen; after all, he hadn't asked for help, or done any special meditations. Nevertheless, my explanation of how the line works must have helped set up his consciousness, and he had read the six words with some degree of earnestness. Thank God he did.

A few minutes later, he received the phone call that all parents dread. It was from his baby's nanny. There had been a car accident; a truck hit a car and it jumped the curb and hit the stroller. The baby was all right; the paramedics only wanted to take her to the hospital as a precaution. We ran—sprinted—the ten blocks to the scene of the accident, and thank God, the baby was fine. A lamppost had stopped the car in its tracks and it only nicked the stroller, breaking an axle, but not the baby's sleep. The car was totaled, but no one was hurt *(Bli ayn hara)*. Subsequent conversation with the nanny and the accident report showed that the accident occurred at precisely the moment Scott was reciting the Genesis Prayer.

Why I was writing about the power of the first line and how it should be used in emergencies at just that moment I don't know. Why Scott had to read the line out loud instead of silently to himself I don't know. Why the accident had to happen in the first place I don't know, either. I do know that both Scott and I both know that it was no coincidence, just as Carmela and her daughter know that her mother's recital of the Genesis Prayer was no coincidence, either. We can dismiss everything in life as pure coincidence and let the chips fall where they may, or we can accept that there's more to life than meets the eye and learn how to stack the odds in our favor.

My wife is reading over my shoulder and reminding me that I should explain why Allison felt it was so important to do the Genesis

Prayer first thing in the morning. The answer is that the purpose of the sages and the Genesis Prayer was to work with the energy of the universe and not against it, what we'd call "going with the flow." Just as the energy of the week works in cycles, so does the energy of the day, month, and year. Each time period is full of wonderful windows of opportunity, just waiting for us to leap through. Some times, however, have more power and potential than others. The most powerful times to do the Genesis Prayer are first thing in the morning—as close to dawn as possible—and again, if you wish, later in the afternoon, shortly before dusk—traditionally a time of judgment—and then again late at night, preferably after midnight. But please do it whenever it feels right for you; the energy around you is a subtle and personal matter, and who better than you to decide what's most appropriate? Whether you take advantage of the specific windows of time or not, the Genesis Prayer will work for you. God willing, you'll be experiencing these miracles for yourself very soon.

CONSCIOUSNESS AND TAXICABS

We've used the Genesis Prayer so many times to help us get through routine trials that we *almost* take it for granted. I emphasize *almost* because one of the keys to successful prayers and meditations is humility. Without appreciation, nothing will work for us. We can't get cocky and forget that we're not the one performing the miracles, we're just the ones requesting them and receiving the benefits. We're only the channels, and the Genesis Prayer is only the gateway for that magnificent, beneficent light force. As we tap into this all-giving, all-sharing force, we need to be cognizant that the gates can shut down in an instant, and that we'd have no one to blame but ourselves because we're the only ones who can turn it on and off; we do it with our consciousness. Think about it: if you didn't thank and/or tip your doorman, how long will it take before he stops smiling at you, before he stops carrying your bags, before he stops opening the door?

The Light Force won't wait long. It's a system of checks and balances; it's a system to teach us cause and effect. When our heads are in the right place, the gates open; when they're not, they're closed. It's simple. It's all about OUR consciousness. The more we are like the Light Force, sharing and loving unconditionally, the more the Light can flow through us, bringing with it all the blessings and miracles that it embodies.

Another couple who do the Genesis Prayer together is Julio and his wife, and when I asked them if they had any Genesis Prayer miracle stories I was overwhelmed with their response; they had dozens and dozens of them, many of which dealt with routine matters, but a couple of tales had unusual twists that help illustrate the extent of the power of the Genesis Prayer. They also show how even though we can't see the big picture, the universe does, and the Genesis Prayer is our window into it.

On one particular taxi trip their driver got into an altercation with a bicycle messenger and it got ugly. Besides cursing each other out in different languages, the messenger was off his bike and pulling at the driver's door as Julio and his wife sat like backseat prisoners trapped behind another car at a red light. Thinking quickly, Julio led them in a rapid Genesis Prayer, and as strange as it seems, once they finished the prayer the messenger stopped pounding and apologized. If I hadn't seen similar incidents myself I'd find it hard to believe, too, but I know them, know the power of the Genesis Prayer, and know it's true. I'm sure what happened was that Julio and his wife slipped into a happier parallel universe, one in which the altercation never occurred and the messenger was sorry for bumping into the cab. Who knows what transpired in the one they left; it wasn't good. Thank God they had the presence of mind to say the Prayer.

Consciousness also comes into play with Natasha's story and how her daily Genesis Prayer changed the consciousness and fortunes for her entire place of business, although she was only an assistant. Natasha, a Russian émigré, was hired to help out a gifted antique furniture restorer who for years had the dream of owning his own gallery. Though successful, his company could never get its act together and move up to the next level. Natasha—Nata to her friends—understood that all objects retain energy and that the antiques the shop was working on had seen much in their long lives, much joy, to be sure, but also many fights and arguments, and even death and murder, so she took it upon herself to clear out the chaotic energy surrounding their business. At first secretively and later with her boss's blessing, Natasha did the Genesis Prayer as she prepared their daily coffee, especially as she poured the water. In no time at all the infighting and the arguments ceased and the business started generating huge profits. Within a year, her boss not only had his dream gallery, but was also named "Businessman of the Year." Even his real estate business thrived. He made sure Natasha alone made their coffee. And just in case we think this a coincidence, less than a year after Natasha left the business, it has fallen back into disarray. She made it very clear to me that her boss's success had nothing to do with her own business acumen or any special talent of her own, other than her spiritual fervor and desire to help her employer and co-workers by using the Genesis Prayer.

4

All Is Not Lost

SECOND CHANCES

As Allison found out, the Genesis Prayer gives us a second chance and shows us the beneficence of the Light force of God.

Sometimes the Genesis Prayer gives us a second chance without our awareness. We all need second chances. Your child tries to walk, stumbles, and falls, you don't tell him he can't try anymore, God forbid; you keep encouraging him and picking him up until he gets it right. That's what the Genesis Prayer does for us. True, life doesn't seem that way; it often feels like it's just one punishment after another. That feeling will change when you're connected, when you make your presence known, when you acknowledge that you want miracles in your life and that there's a benevolent force out there beyond our comprehension that wants to give miracles to us. The greater our belief in miracles, the more effective the Genesis Prayer will be for us. That's not to say a skeptic won't see them, but if it's something you want, why fight it? You don't start a sales call with your potential customer by saying, "You don't really want to buy anything from me, do you?" Don't communicate with the universe that way, either. Why push away all that beneficence? You're simply making things difficult for yourself and your family.

Graham, a British architect whose ex-wife moved to California with their son, was a believer. He got his second chance. He was traveling from New York's LaGuardia Airport to Los Angeles via a connection in Chicago, and his connecting time was too close for comfort. He had a feeling he might have trouble making the second plane, but there were no other reasonably priced flights. If time was tight, money was tighter. He had to see his son, but he had limited resources to spend doing so.

Technical delays at the gate made the schedule even tighter, chewing away at any leeway he may have had. When the engines shut down on the tarmac, the plane came to a halt, and the lights shut off, he knew he'd run out of luck. He knew he'd never make his connection nor see his son; and who knew when he'd get the opportunity again? The pilot announced they'd be back in the take-off line in an hour, too late for Graham, especially since he'd flown enough to know the pilot was being optimistic and that the taxiing line at LaGuardia could be quite long in itself. Most passengers cursed or took advantage of the darkness to catch some shuteye. Graham took matters into his own hands; he did the Genesis Prayer. As he recited the meditation and scanned the appropriate angels of the day, he asked for help getting to Chicago on time to catch his connecting flight on to L.A. Not a minute later, the lights went back on and the engines fired up. The sixteen planes ahead of them were mysteriously down to two and he arrived in L.A. in time to spend the weekend reacquainting and bonding with his son. They got their second chance.

There were no explanations from the pilot, no word of what happened to the other fourteen planes, but Graham already knew. The situation for Graham and his flight had been changed. Something shifted when Graham did the Genesis Prayer, and once again life was good. He'd seen it happen before, and he knew he'd see it again.

The Genesis Prayer brought Sammy a second chance, but in a different way. He'd recently moved to California and had been out hiking with friends in the snow-covered mountains east of L.A.

Before they knew it, darkness had descended upon them. They'd been hiking off-trail, as stupid as that sounds, but still they made it back down the wooded snowbound slope and managed to find their car. What Sammy couldn't find was his keys—to his car, apartment, storage locker, and a half dozen other things. Looking up into the blustery darkness, his heart sank—his whole life was inaccessible without those keys, not to mention having to abandon his car and find a way back to the city in the cold of the night. The slope got bigger and wider and the forest deeper and more impenetrable as he second-guessed his decision to pack up everything and move out west. He was always losing stuff and never recovered it—even in his own apartment! They all knew it would be impossible to find those keys before the summer meltoff—if even then—yet they trudged back up the hill. Although they even found one of the spots where they'd pulled up to rest, no keys. If you've ever dropped anything into a snowbank, you know it could have been right in front of them, two feet down and an icy world away. In all probability, the keys would have sunk into the snow without leaving even a trace on the surface—such is the nature of snow. They'd been hiking for hours that evening. It was futile. It was then that Sammy's friend Ben suggested the Genesis Prayer. He'd never heard of anyone using it for finding lost articles, but he knew it brought miracles to all who asked for help. What did they have to lose? They all did the prayer together, and not two minutes later, something made Sammy stop along the side of their path of footprints and dig beneath the snow. Sure enough, there were his keys.

There had been no sign from heaven, no gap in the snow, no break in their footprints, only a voice in his head, only the Genesis Prayer doing its work.

Was it a miracle? Of course, but the following week, Sammy had the occasion to share his good fortune and pass on the benefits of the Genesis Prayer to another friend as Ben had for him. Meeting a friend at the Santa Monica beach, Sammy was greeted with a very long face. His friend had lost his reading glasses somewhere in the sand. It's about a five-minute walk from the promenade to the water, and Sammy's friend had cut across on a diagonal, so he wasn't sure where he'd walked. But Sammy had confidence in the Prayer thanks to his experience with his keys in the snow. Reciting the Genesis Prayer for them, he was infused with the powers of intuition and heightened perception that the ancient *Zohar* tells us can be gleamed from the prayer's fifth line. Like a man on a mission, Sammy marched straight out into the sand and came back a few minutes later with the glasses.

His friend, dumbfounded, became a believer.

HELP IN A CRISIS

Someone who was out of time and wouldn't have gotten a second chance was Miri, a twenty-five-year-old Israeli girl, recently emigrated to the United States. She had promised her Orthodox rabbi's wife that she'd have her new custom-made $2,000 dress in time for the Rosh Hashanah holiday, the Jewish New Year and one of the holiest days of the year, and for a rabbi's wife the most important day to shine with new clothes.

Miri came from a long line of couture tailors dating back farther than anyone remembered, and though her specialty was sales, her design training was what inspired her to volunteer her family's services. The rabbi's wife and Miri had been through magazines, catalogues, and countless sketches and fabric swatches together and were sure they'd designed the perfect dress: understated, but oh so elegant.

An Orthodox woman doesn't get too many opportunities to show off and radiate outside her home, so the rabbi's wife particularly wanted to look good on this occasion, especially because her family and friends were flying in from all over, not to mention a thousand members of their congregation. She was counting on Miri to come through for her.

It was Friday morning, and the holiday would begin at sunset that evening and the dress had not yet arrived. Desperate, Miri had managed to get a call through to her family in Israel just before they entered the holiday and thus became unreachable for the next two days. They confirmed that the dress had been sent by U.P.S., but they couldn't find the tracking number.

Making matters worse, an influential member of the congregation had donated the dress and had already paid for it. Not only would he feel terrible if his rabbi's wife attended services wearing the same dress she'd worn all year, but he might even feel duped by her, or feel that *he* was the cause of her embarrassment. Worse yet, everyone knew that the last thing the rabbi needed was for his wife to be upset while he tried to make the highest connections for his congregation, ones that influenced greatly their entire year, and ones that he'd been meditating on nonstop for three days in preparation for the holiday. Miri shuddered as she thought about the repercussions if she were unable to locate the dress.

Frantic, she ran to the nearest U.P.S. office, but there was nothing they could do without a number. They did suggest, though, that she might try tracking down her local U.P.S. truck and ask the driver if he'd check his cargo for her. In Manhattan that meant spending the last hours before the two-day high holiday running up and down 52nd, 53rd, 54th, 55th and 56th Streets, which she did, of course—what choice did she have? It was to no avail. It was well past noon, and there were only a few hours left before she'd have to give up and leave for the hotel the congregation had rented out for the holiday, thus abandoning all hope of finding the dress. Once the holiday began, she'd have to break the religious laws of both it and the Sabbath to use the phone or even sign for the package, and even if she did, the rabbi's wife would never accept it on those terms; she'd rather do without than have Miri or anyone break the holiday laws on her account. Miri was in trouble.

U.P.S. trucks are easy to spot; they're chocolate brown. But it was not as easy as Miri thought. She found plenty of FedEx trucks, mail trucks, even a DHL truck, but for whatever reason, the U.P.S. ones were avoiding her. How long could she keep searching? She still had to prepare for the holiday. Assuming she could find the truck, she had no way of knowing if it was the right one, or even if the package had arrived in the United States. It could be at the airport, at Customs, at a distribution center, or still in Israel for all she knew. Her parents had said it was supposed to arrive in the morning, but it hadn't. It was hours past due.

Luckily for Miri, her uncle was helping her and, more important than sharing the searching burden, he suggested they try the Genesis Prayer together. There is a special property of the Genesis Prayer that makes it stronger when done with others with a single purpose. Its structure, which we'll get into later, is designed for unification and unity, to bring people closer together, to create a oneness with the universe and within society; it's a beautiful side effect of doing the prayer with consciousness. One whole line is dedicated to establishing human dignity and world peace.

They did as he suggested. Suddenly they spotted the familiar brown truck that had eluded them all morning.

The truck was parked outside an office building on 54th, a fifty-story tower, and the concierge had no clue what floor the driver was on. Not knowing whether to be happy or to cry, Miri took the elevator to the top floor. Dejected, she repeated to herself, "fifty floors to search."

While her uncle waited by the truck, lest they miss the driver, she frantically ran from floor to floor, checking all the offices, asking passersby if they'd seen the man in the brown uniform. After about four floors she realized the futility of her task and returned in tears to her uncle. With all the offices to check and doors to knock on, each one panicked her more. The driver could have been anywhere, and Miri knew it could easily take another hour before he finished all his stops in the building. She didn't have an hour. She glared at her watch—not ten minutes to spare; they'd wasted the entire day. They could just wait by the truck, but if the driver didn't appear within the next few minutes, it wouldn't matter because they'd have to leave to get to the hotel in time for the holiday. With her uncle's arm around her shoulder, they did the Genesis Prayer again, one last time before giving up and heading to the hotel. That's when the elevator *binged* and the driver stepped out.

He didn't have it with him, though. He didn't have it in his truck, either. Sympathetic to their plight, he checked all the packages out for delivery that day. Nothing.

Before he let the driver leave, Miri's uncle had them try the Genesis Prayer one more time as the driver looked on. Suddenly it occurred to the driver to check yet one more area of the truck that was set aside for night deliveries. Sure enough, it was there, marked erroneously for delivery that night, too late for the holiday. He watched, smiling, as Miri signed for the package.

Her persistence paid off. We never know what forces are lined up against us, what we've done to deserve the trials and tribulations we're subjected to each and every day, or how we will be tested and what hoops we have to jump through to accomplish our tasks. It seems that the more enlightened and spiritual our task, the more obstacles are lined up against us. We've all experienced good turns and deeds that backfired. Nevertheless, it was Miri's and her uncle's persistent use of and belief in the Genesis Prayer that really paid off for them. Only the Genesis Prayer has the ability to blast through all the accumulated negativity in our world, lives, and karma. And as we saw with Miri's dilemma, sometimes it takes more than one meditation, but we can't give up our faith, not if our intentions are pure. All the bad that could have come from Miri's failure weighed against her success. Over a thousand people's lives for the coming year depended on her coming through for the rabbi's wife. It doesn't matter whether we believe this to be true or not; Miri did.

If at any time in the process she had said, "Enough, I can't go on," or "It's impossible, screw it," she would have failed. Who knows how bad the consequences would have been, but in Miri's mind they would have been catastrophic. The Genesis Prayer gave her just enough hope to get to the next step. It didn't eliminate the process, the test, entirely, but gave her mercy, making it easier for her. It gave her the strength to continue and to overcome.

How many of us are going through that process right now: with health, with our children, with relationships, with work, with finances, with our fears of terrorism, or just with the chaos and stress of our everyday lives? Don't we all need encouragement? Don't we all need help? Something to make it through to the next step and give us the breathing room to think things through, to work them through? To help us find our faith? Wouldn't it be nice if, like Miri, we could stick it through to the end? Wouldn't it be nice if we had a tool, like the Genesis Prayer, to make things work out in the end?

Bli ayn hara, Miri got her wish and got to learn things about herself as well by going through a process. We're going to go through the processes anyway, so why not win in the end?

5

Everyday Miracles

TOM'S CAT

The varied uses and the miracles produced by the Genesis Prayer never cease to amaze me. Tom was explaining to me the other morning why I hadn't seen him for morning prayers in a while. He'd been too tired. Tom and his wife have three cats, the youngest of which, Tiferet, had been keeping them up all night with his constant crying. "It was unending, every night, all night, nothing worked." He'd tried everything, and every day they were more tired, more exhausted, and more unnerved.

So with nothing to lose, Tom tried the meditations on his cat, including the optional *Tikune HaNefesh* healing meditation. That night they all slept like babies—straight through, with not a peep out of little Tiferet.

"It's been three days and I feel wonderful," he reported. They've been repeating the meditation every night with the same wonderful results *(Bli ayn hara)*, which was why Tom is back praying with us in the morning.

I'd never read about anyone using the Genesis Prayer on animals before, but as Tom's cat proved, why not? The Genesis Prayer works because of quantum technology, and since according to both our scientists and the ancient sages we're all connected at the subatomic level, all a part of a greater whole, why shouldn't the Genesis Prayer and Tom's positive consciousness affect his cat? Or his plants, for that matter? We all know our moods affect our pets as easily as they do our families and, according to many studies, our plants as well. Moreover, according to the sages, the Bible goes to great lengths to teach us that our speech and consciousness affect the walls of our homes, too, so why not use the Genesis Prayer to reverse all that? The sages did; they often cleansed their homes of negativity by reciting the Genesis Prayer. The Bible speaks of sick buildings and of destroying infected walls, and what the sages call the results of our negative consciousness, our scientists call quantum transference. With all matter exchanging energy on a quantum or subatomic level, how could our homes and its contents not pick up on our vibes? Nevertheless, as illustrated by Tom's cat and Natasha's meditations over her office's coffee, the Genesis Prayer can inject a positive force into anything or anyone. All we need to do is stretch our imaginations; the Genesis Prayer will take care of the rest.

NO ONE LOSES

Martha's experience with the Genesis Prayer was a little different. She never knew it was being done for her. One summer day a few years ago Martha slipped and broke her hip. The pain was excruciating, and after being rushed to the hospital she was administered many drugs, but other than make her groggy the drugs did little for the pain that seemed to pierce every fiber of her being. That night, before her daughter could reach the hospital, Martha went into cardiac arrest. Her husband watched helplessly as she paled, blued, and flatlined all in a matter of seconds. The crash team revived her, but she was even groggier than before.

By the time Martha's daughter arrived, the crisis was over, but now the problem was that the doctors couldn't operate. In the best of circumstances hip replacement is a major traumatic surgery, but in Martha's condition the doctors felt it would be fatal. That didn't leave Martha with many options.

It was decided to run multiple tests to see how bad her heart was. They weren't optimistic. In fact, they weren't interested in seeing if she could have her hip surgery; they needed to know which heart procedure to do. Martha's daughter began doing the Genesis Prayer at once. Martha's a huge skeptic, but she was so out of it she had no idea what her daughter was up to.

Each test was more invasive than the next. Each time, Martha's daughter dutifully performed the Genesis Prayer during the entire test. One by one, the test results came back negative. Then came the most invasive one of all, when they had to thread a catheter through Martha's artery and up into her heart. The surgeons were already scrubbing up and everyone was waiting to see how bad the damage was and what shape her arteries were in. They shook their heads: obviously, the earlier tests were flawed.

All through the half-hour test Martha had had the Genesis Prayer done for her, including the special optional *Tikune HaNefesh* healing meditation. Over and over, her daughter concentrated the blessings on her mother's heart. Finally, they pulled the catheter out and wheeled Martha back to intensive care.

Not one, but three doctors came to give Martha's husband and daughter the lowdown. The family braced for the worst, gripping each other's hands like claws. The baffled doctors could only shake their heads, admitting they couldn't find anything wrong with Martha's heart whatsoever: no clogging, no scarring, no signs she'd ever had a heart attack or ever had a reason to have had one. They were dumbfounded. They saw the attack with their own eyes, saw the monitor flatline, but now there was nothing, no indications Martha had ever had anything wrong with her other than a broken hip.

It was decided to proceed with the hip replacement surgery, and once again Martha had the Genesis Prayer repeatedly recited for her. Two years later she's back on the golf course. *Bli ayn hara.*

I don't think Martha ever knew what her daughter or the Genesis Prayer had done for her, but that didn't matter to the universe. It was her daughter who had done the work and who had the faith. She didn't do it to get something in return, only for the health of her mother. It was a selfless act full of love. No, it didn't take a huge sacrifice on her part, only faith, but that's all it's supposed to take. A month later Martha's daughter met her soul mate and was married in the spring. *Bli ayn hara.*

When we pray for others, we get more in return; it's a basic tenet of the spiritual universe. By making ourselves a channel for the Light Force of the Creator to flow through us, we benefit even more than the recipient of our prayers, who benefits as well. That's why it's so beautiful. No one loses. That's the difference between letting the Genesis Prayer connect us to the limitless spiritual realm and us battling for change in our world.

WE ALL HAVE TO START SOMEWHERE

Miri, and even more so her uncle, were believers in the Genesis Prayer already, as were Carmela, Julio, Natasha, Allison, my wife and I, Andrea and her husband, Scott, Sammy's friend, Graham, Tom, and Martha's daughter, but what about someone who's a little skeptical? What if they're only trying because they think, "What do I have to lose?"

That's what was going through Dr. Wallace's head when she ran into a brick wall while buying a computer for her office. She was under a lot of pressure to get the right computer and get it right away, yesterday if possible. This technical area wasn't her forte, but after much consternation she felt she'd chosen the perfect computer for their needs. After protracted negotiating over the price, the salesman checked his inventory and found that the model they'd selected was out of stock. Dr. Wallace would have to either wait a couple weeks or start searching all over again. She thought, "Why not try the *Ana B'ko'ack*?" and sure enough, a physical search of the warehouse turned up her model, even though no one remembered one being there and the store's usually reliable inventory system showed the model as definitely out of stock.

Elated, Dr. Wallace paid for the system and made arrangements for delivery, but no one was available. All the delivery trucks were out, and their schedules were already full. She had to wait. "Why not?" she thought, and tried the Genesis Prayer again.

How, why? She didn't know or care, but a deliveryman called in to say he was heading back to the store because a delivery just got canceled. The salesman, of course, informed her that it must be her lucky day. That assessment changed when she needed to have the computer set up and installed. Once again, no one was available.

Once again Dr. Wallace did the Genesis Prayer. And once again, miraculously, an installer called in, asking if there was any work available. Three tries, three miracles. Dr. Wallace was convinced. Her medical training had taught her to accept, in principle, mind over matter, the placebo affect, the benefits of a positive outlook on healing, and that some patients have been able to will themselves better. She'd even seen multiple studies, such as the Columbia University pregnancy meditation in which people prayed for a specific group of women, whom they didn't know, to help them get pregnant and these women actually got pregnant at a much higher rate than they would have otherwise. It was a double-blind study in that these women were not only halfway across the globe in Korea, but they didn't know anyone was praying for them at the time. There are many studies of this type whispered about in the medical community, but none of them do anything close to what the Genesis Prayer does.

What Dr. Wallace witnessed firsthand had gone beyond what was discussed in alternative medicine, went beyond the practices of Oriental medicine, went beyond the laws of physics. Things, like her computer, seemed to pop into being from out of nowhere. People called in or appeared who weren't even contacted, entire series of events took place beyond their stream of consciousness, all to allow her computer to be installed that day. It makes you wonder, if the Genesis Prayer can work like this on computers, what could it do for modern medicine? It's ancient therapy that my teacher refers to as twenty-fifth-century technology.

Today it looks like magic, but what would cell phones have looked like just two hundred years ago? How about computers or lightbulbs?

Speaking of cell phones, we don't really have to know how they work in order to use them, do we? As long as the connection is made, most of us are content with dialing the number and letting the technology do its thing. The Genesis Prayer works like that, too—as long as we get our miracles, why should we care how the connection was made?

Nevertheless, we're all skeptical to one degree or another; we all need convincing. It's our nature. But with the Genesis Prayer, it's just a matter of trying it. That's all that's left. In the next few sections we'll explain how the meditations work, and in Part VI why they work—their origins, physical and metaphysical.

6

42 *Letters That Add Up to Miracles*

M<small>Y WIFE AND I DEBATED OVER AND OVER WHICH PART TO</small> include first, the section on the meditation or the one explaining its underlying codes. The codes *are* what make the meditations work, but in the end we decided it's the *miracles* that we're really after. I mean, what's more important—knowing how the cell phone transmits messages, or getting them? Or as my wife put it, "Do you want the blueprints or the house?" So deferring to my wife's better judgment, we put most of the proofs toward the back of book, and let the Genesis Prayer speak for itself.

The Genesis Prayer, or in Hebrew/Aramaic, the *Ana B'ko'ack*, is a simple meditation built around a scaffolding of **42** letters that correspond with the first **42** letters of the Bible and also with the **42** places the Israelites stopped at in their journey through the desert. In the verses Numbers 33:1–49 the Bible synopsizes their **42**-stop journey to and from each place, and in Hebrew the words "to" and "from" are prefixes attached to the names of the places themselves. And not by coincidence, the prefix *mem* (מ) for "from" and *bet* (ב) for "to" are alternatively used to describe the long journey, with the numerical value for *mem* being 40 and for *bet* being 2, or together, **42**, which is why the sages refer to the Genesis Prayer as the "*Mem-Bet*," the **42**-letter Name. (The numerical values are based on the ancient Hebrew counting system.) Both the Bible and the Genesis Prayer are marvels of engineering, with each letter having a specific numerical value, thus allowing the entire Bible or any section of it to be examined in purely mathematical terms, removing much of the subjectivity associated with interpretation. As we recite the words associated with the **42** letters, we're mimicking that **42**-place journey from the darkness of exile and into the Light; we're sharing their spiritual process. The miracle is that the Genesis Prayer's complex codes make it happen within a few minutes, as opposed to the 40 years that the Israelites endured.

The **42** words that correspond to the **42** letters are also coded, thus reinforcing the power of the **42** letters, which is why they must be pronounced in the original Hebrew and Aramaic. Because the Genesis Prayer, like the entire Pentateuch, or *Five Books of Moses,* was given to the seventy nations of the world at Mt. Sinai, it makes no difference if we read from a transliterated version because the pronunciation is the same as the Hebrew/Aramaic one. Most everyone I know, and nearly all those in our miracle stories, used the easy-to-read transliterated version.

We know from the sages that the Torah and the Genesis Prayer were meant for the seventy nations all along, and we've included additional proof of this in Part VI. For the moment, we can note that the **42** letters—the basis and core of the prayer—form the beginning letters of **42** words, which thus guides us to properly pronounce the letters with their correct intonations. These **42** words, which form the full Genesis Prayer, have a total of 175 letters, corresponding to the 175 years of Abraham, the father of Christianity, Judaism, and Islam, and a direct link to the seventy nations. This concept is very important because the Genesis Prayer is a unifying force, a force that can bring together all the nations of the world. As will be explained later, the first line and also the final one connect us to Abraham as well, and thus it's said that the Genesis Prayer brings together these three major religions born of Abraham, brings them back to a time of spirituality and of oneness with the Creator. It's said that if we connect with our roots through the Genesis Prayer and Abraham we can spiritually transport back before the dawn of religion, back before Moses and the seventy Nations received the Torah, back thirty-eight hundred years to when God spoke directly with Abraham.

It's the separation we experience in our lives that blocks the miracles. We must want to be one soul with our fellow man. But saying it and doing it are quite different things, and since none of us are saints, the universe gives us some leeway: if we have at least the intention in our hearts, our consciousness will follow.

As will be explained in detail, the Genesis Prayer is the **42** letters and their associated meditations that help guide the miracles to specific areas of our lives. The words themselves are simply vehicles to get those **42** letters into our consciousness, so their translation, while poetic, is not nearly as significant as the mediations that we'll soon learn. The following is the strict English translation without the guiding meditations:

> We beg Thee,
> with the strength and greatness of Thy
> right arm, untangle our knotted fate.
>
> Accept your people's song,
> elevate and purify us, oh Awesome One.
>
> Please, Heroic One,
> those who pursue Your Uniqueness—
> guard them as the pupil of an eye.
>
> Bless them, purify them, pity them,
> May Your righteousness always reward them.
>
> Powerful and Holy One,
> In goodness lead Your flock.
> Unique and Proud One,
> turn to Your people, who remember Your holiness.

Accept our cries,
and hear our screams,
oh Knower of mysteries.

(Blessed is the Name of His Noble Kingdom forever and ever.)

As we can plainly see, this poem is beseeching God to hear us and to answer us with miracles, but if we were to recite it in English it would lose all the power and meditative properties encoded in the original form. So it should suffice to know what we're saying, but beyond that, the English version has no more effect than any other prayer. The transliterated version, though, is different. Since we're pronouncing the words, it's as if we were reciting the prayer in its original Hebrew/Aramaic state. And if we make a visual connection while we do it, it's even better than knowing either Hebrew or Aramaic, which share the same alphabet, because the extra effort we're putting in to pronounce words and sounds that are unfamiliar to us tells the cosmos we mean business. Going the extra mile is what spirituality is all about; when we do, we're creating angels for ourselves. Not angels with wings per se, but quantum messengers.

It's important to note that the essence of the prayer is the **42** letters derived from the first **42** letters of Genesis and that the transliterated words we recite are there only for us to be able to invoke those **42** letters with the proper intonation and vowel pronunciation. By themselves they serve little higher purpose and even less in their English translation.

FLIGHT OF THE ANGELS

In centuries past, the depiction of angels flying back and forth from heaven on high was both beautiful and appropriate, considering the populace's knowledge of physics and the universe, but today we know much more. Today, we can understand angels as subatomic particles operating at speeds far greater than the speed of light, and thus from our point of view they're not particles or energy, but both. Moreover, they're quantum bundles capable of being imprinted and of carrying those imprinted messages instantly to the far corners of the universe. Because they operate faster than light, much faster, our perception of their transference of information happens instantly. As we can read in the headlines, our scientists are trying to tap into this cosmic process to create computers unencumbered by chips and hardware. My guess is that it will take a while, but be that as it may, what these angelic messengers are really imprinting are not the on/off switches of binary computer code, but our own codes: our thoughts, graphic 3D and 4D holographic images of our actions, good and bad—our consciousness.

Nothing we think or do goes unnoticed by the cosmos. Nothing we think or do happens in a vacuum; it all has an effect on the universe. For better or worse, we're constantly projecting these messages, broadcasting to the universe and to all who live in it who we really are, what we really think, and what type of energy and people we want to attract into our lives. It's for this reason that we need to take advantage of every opportunity to create positive quantum angels. It's for this reason that we need to tap into an angel-producing source like the Genesis Prayer as often as we can. Unless our thoughts and actions are pure, and it's doubtful many of us are saints, we need all the help we can get to generate and broadcast *positivity* into the universe. Remember, what we project, we attract. Opposites attract only in magnets. In spirituality we get what we give.

THE PRINCIPLE OF AFFINITY

Getting what we give is called the principle of affinity. Because our actions and thoughts are broadcast to the far reaches of the universe, we're telling everyone in the universe what we think, feel, and do—who we really are. This is why, no matter what façade we put on, people see right through us. The only ones we are really fooling are ourselves. It's also why people who think like us, or who are at the same level of consciousness as us, suddenly appear in our lives. Unconsciously, we're attracting them. So if our thoughts are good and pure, we'll attract more spiritual people to ourselves, who help us get to an even higher level of spirituality.

The flip side is also true. If our thoughts aren't so pure, neither will be those individuals who gather around us, thus making it harder for us to break out of our spiritual morass. This isn't necessarily bad, because by seeing our own thoughts and actions in others, we're given the opportunity to recognize and deal with that negativity face to face. Otherwise, we may never recognize it for what it is, and we will continue to be forced to wrestle with it internally.

Fortunately, the Genesis Prayer acts as our advocate to the universe, standing by our side, helping to keep us from incriminating ourselves as it continually argues on our behalf, helping to cleanse and buffer that negativity before we broadcast it. It's *so* much more powerful than we can imagine.

PART III

THE GENESIS PRAYER
(OR *ANA B'KO'ACK*)
MEDITATION

7

The Ten Dimensions

THE **42** LETTERS THAT ARE DERIVED FROM THE FIRST **42** letters of the Bible are the first letters in the **42** words of the original Hebrew Genesis Prayer. These **42** words are split into seven lines of six words each, with each of those seven lines acting as a gateway to a different dimension or energy level and, as the sages explain, each line broadcasting to all six directions—north, south, east, west, up, and down. Just as the electricity that enters our lamps at home starts out at very powerful voltage levels and must be stepped down several times before it's usable for us, so, too, is the energy we're tapping into with the Genesis Prayer.

The first verse in the Bible reads:

> In the beginning of God's creation of heaven and earth, the earth was without form and empty.[1] (Genesis 1:1)

In Abraham's *Sefer Yetzirah, The Book of Formation,* written four hundred years earlier than the Torah, he describes "10 *sefirot* of nothingness," which the sages tell us corresponds to the emptiness

---

[1] The commonly accepted and most prevalent translation from the original Hebrew by the eleventh-century sage Rashi. Others translate it as, "In the beginning God created heaven and earth. The earth was without form and empty . . ."

that existed before earth had form—it existed in a state of potential. By *potential* we mean that it was fully imprinted in the upper dimensions, but not as yet projected onto our four-dimensional world—kind of like existing in our imagination before we tell anyone what we're thinking. We live in a world of three dimensions plus, as Einstein taught us, the fourth dimension, that of spacetime. We don't need to comprehend these upper dimensions, those above our four-dimensional lives; we only need to know that Abraham and the sages agreed with today's physicists on the matter, and that the seven dimensions we're going to tap into in the Genesis Prayer are from highest to lowest:

Chesed	7
Gevurah	6
Tiferet	5
Netzach	4
Hod	3
Yesod	2
Malckut	**1**

These seven dimensions each have special attributes, which we sum up in single words such as *mercy* and *strength,* and as we explain the Genesis Prayer line by line, we'll be defining them in terms of their relevance to their corresponding lines. If you must visualize them, you can try picturing them as seven concentric spheres, all separate, yet all part of a whole, and in that scenario we and our dimension, called *Malckut,* would be in the center. The sages tell us, however, that any attempt to visualize them limits their effect on us because instead of letting the universe take care of us, we're screening its desires through our personal perception. The only thing important to know is that they're activated in descending order and that all the energy and blessings of the outer ones get absorbed and transformed level by level until it gets funneled down to us through the penultimate one, the second one from the bottom, *Yesod,* and into our world, the dimension of *Malckut,* "the earthly kingdom."

Each one of the levels is also associated with a different patriarch, as will be explained line by line, each with their own attributes that can be imparted to us. One of the important principles to be aware of is that the merit of each patriarch is cumulative as we drop down from level to level, meaning that our blessings are increased exponentially as we unconsciously process their distinct energies.

The Hebrew and Aramaic languages are read from right to left as opposed to English, which is read left to right, and even in transliterated form this takes some getting used to, so we're going to first present it as if you were reading regular English and then we'll do it again in its original form.

Left to Right →

> *Ana B'ko'ack Gedulat Yeminechah Tatir Tsrurah*
> *Kahbel Rinat Amechah Sagvenu Taharenu Norah*
> *Na Gibor Dorshay Yichudechah Kevavat Shomrem*
> *Barckem Taharem Rackamay Tsidkatechah Tamid Gomlem*
> *Khasin Kadosh Berov Tuvchah Nahel Adatechah*
> *Yackid Geh'eh L'amcha P'nay Zockray K'dushatechah*
> *Shavatenu Kahbel Ushma Tsa'akatenu Yode'ah Ta'alumot*
> *(Baruch Shem Kevod Malckutoh L'olam Va'ed)*

Note: The "k" in the transliterated words above is pronounced as a gutteral "h," as in *house*. It's kind of like the "J" in the Spanish *José*. Also, the emphasis is always on the last syllable.

The last line in parentheses is a special code that is whispered. It seals off and protects the meditation. It also helps us to ground and manifest all the energy we've received.

Even if the miracles don't happen for us instantaneously—and, of course, many times they will—by doing the Genesis Prayer properly, we're actually drawing down the energy with which the miracles in our world are created. The potential is there for us at once, but sometimes it takes a little longer to manifest. Remember, we don't see the big (complete) picture and we don't even know what's best for us, so it's possible that by doing the Genesis Prayer, a miracle will occur for us and we won't realize it, or we'll find out about it later, as Carmela did with her daughter's accident. All the more reason to do it more often! This is no cop-out; by doing the Genesis Prayer you *will* see the miracles, just not every time. Miracles happen, most of us already know it, but we also know people who pooh-pooh that notion and don't even see the miracles when they themselves are the recipients. We've all been in that dark place where we couldn't see anything good in anything, and dismissed any miracles that befell us as coincidence. The Genesis Prayer makes miracles happen more often, but what we're thinking and feeling—our consciousness—has a lot to do with what miracles we'll actually see. If miracles happen and we repeatedly deny their existence, the universe will have no reason to keep creating them for us. On the other hand, the more appreciative we are, the more miracles we'll see and the more often we'll see them. The better the place we find ourselves in spiritually, and the more we're working on ourselves and on our consciousness, the bigger and more obvious the miracles will be. When we elevate our consciousness above the fog and din of our world—something the Genesis Prayer is particularly good at doing—we begin to see things for what they really are.

When we recite the Genesis Prayer, we split the six words on each line into three columns—right, left, and central—corresponding to the three dimensions of our world and to the positive, negative, and neutral forces that exist in nature and spirituality. The neutral force is also known as the resistive one, or simply as resistance. The proton, electron, and neutron come to mind, but it's easier to picture this resistance as the resistive filament that lies between the positive and negative poles in a lightbulb. If we put the two ends together like some of us have done accidentally while jump-starting a car, we'd get a spark and blow out the bulb, but by having that filament in between, we get the benefit of the completed circuit of energy, which results in light. Another way to visualize it is like mixing fire and water; they extinguish one another, but if we use a neutral vessel between them, like a pot, we can benefit from the energy flow from the fire to the water, and get hot water.

There's no special meditating to do; the three-column arrangement of the words on the page does all that work for us. As with an arch, whose weight is mostly supported by the central lintel, so, too, are the words in the prayer. The evidence of this is found in the numerical value for the central column of the prayer. There is a well-known ancient practice used extensively by the sages called *gematria,* in which the letters are assigned fixed values based on their underlying energy frequencies (vibrations), and just like energy waves, they can be added or multiplied to produce word values that can be compared and/or connected to other spiritual terms. The sum of the *gematria* values for the fourteen central letters of the Genesis Prayer is the same as the sum of all the integers through **42** (i.e., $42 + 41 + 40 + 39 \ldots$), which means the whole power of the **42** letters is reflected in the central column alone.

In Part VI we'll cover in more detail the workings of the ancient *gematria* ciphers used to interpret the letters and of the special significance of each of these numbers being revealed to us through the coded prayer. For now, we're using them as illustrative tools to understand the complex beauty of this prayer and how it works to help us.

In Appendix Two, we can find a list of the letters of the Hebrew/Aramaic alphabet with their numerical equivalents in three of the more significant *gematria* ciphers as taught to us by the sages. When we explore the workings of the universe and the hidden codes within the ancient texts, we're like blind men tapping our long white canes along the sidewalks of the city: we may slowly find our way, but we can never fully appreciate the beauty that surrounds us. The sages have provided us a way, teaching us to use the numbers as guides. They liken the enormous energy centers of the universe to icebergs: giant hidden storehouses of energy floating beneath the surface of our dimension, whose barely visible tips are the ancient letters themselves. They further explain that the numbers are the imprints that these icebergs make as they slice through the proverbial waters we call space-time. Because we can't read or see the energy vortices themselves, and the letters are too one-dimensional for us to fully grasp, we rely on the numbers to reflect what lies beneath.

In the most basic sense, the way it works is that each letter has been assigned a specific value, and when we sum up the values for all the letters in a word, we get a specific value for that word, which we can then use to compare the word with other known words that have been deigned to have special spiritual significance. Nevertheless, because many words have similar values, instead of making up connections as we find convenient, we default to what the sages have already stated. This may be limiting, but it insures that we don't go askew of the documents' original intentions. Moreover, there is far from an endless list of values to choose from, as one might assume: Of the 79,976 words in the Pentateuch, there are only 1,024 different word values.

We do, though, have many more computational tools at our disposal today and thus can find many more figures with which to draw the comparisons, but no matter how deep we look, the same few significant values keep reappearing, thus reassuring ourselves that the sages knew what they were doing. Just as an illustration of the revelatory power of *gematria* and of the intricate technology built into the Pentateuch, the square root of those 79,976 words is 282.8002828, and according to the sages 28 is not only the primordial number upon which the entire Pentateuch is based, as witnessed by the 28 letters that comprise its first verse, but its meanings when translated into words are "Power," "By God," "Union with God," and "Unity." And in similar fashion to there being precisely 5^8 words, letters, and verses in the 5 Books, the 1,024 different word values is equivalent to exactly 2^{10}, which we're told connects us all to the 210 years that the Israelites were in exile in Egypt.

As is evident, there is much more than meets the eye going on in the Pentateuch, commonly known as the Torah, but what's relevant for us now is the technology built into the Genesis Prayer, which is derived directly from the first **42** letters of the Bible.

Interestingly enough, when we use small *gematria*,[2] another powerful revelatory cipher, to glimpse into the codes, the total value for the two triplets of the sixth line, that of *Yesod,* the funneling dimension, also equals that same summation of all the integers through **42** (i.e., 42 + 41 + 40 + 39 . . .). When numbers add up in this spectacular fashion it's never a coincidence, and when it happens more than once within the same small set of **42** letters it implies a very purposeful design. So it's odder yet that the last triplet of the last line, the *Malckut* level, and thus the final one of the entire Genesis Prayer, is also that same sum of all the integers through **42**. What all this means for us is that the meditation is acting like an energy capacitor. The central column boosts the amount of energy as it descends, and the sixth line boosts it yet again as it funnels it down to the *Malckut* level, where we can take advantage of it. So even though the voltage has decreased to the point where we can handle it, there is much more of it for us to plug into. In other words, just in case our consciousness wasn't strong enough, the meditative mechanism boosts it one last time before we put it out there into the cosmos.

The triplets referred to in the previous paragraph are specific enhancing meditations we do as we recite the Genesis Prayer. The **42** letters are divided into fourteen triplets, which simply means that the six letters associated with each line are broken down into two sets of three letters each for meditative purposes, repeated at the end of each line as follows:

---

[2] *Gematria katan,* or "small *gematria,*" is a most revelatory cipher in which the letter's values are reduced to single digits and then the letters of a word are converted into a string of numbers, similar to computer code, thus giving each word a particular fingerprint.

←Read from Right to Left

	← Left Column	← Central Column	← Right Column	←
אבג יתצ	Tsrurah Tatir	Yeminechah Gedulat	B'ko'ack Ana	Chese(Line 1
קרע שטנ	Norah Taharenu	Sagvenu Amechah	Rinat Kahbel	Gevur(Line 2
נגד יכש	Shomrem Kevavat	Yichudechah Dorshay	Gibor Na	Tiferet Line 3
בטר צתג	Gomlem Tamid	Tsidkatechah Rachamay	Taharem Barckem	Netza(Line 4
חקב טנע	Adatechah Nahel	Tuvchah Berov	Kadosh Khasin	Hod Line 5
יגל פזק	K'dushatechah Zockray	P'nay L'amcha	Geh'eh Yackid	Yesod Line 6
שקו צית	Ta'alumot Yode'ah	Tsa'akatenu Ushma	Kahbel Shavatenu	Malck(Line 7

←(Va'ed L'olam Malckutoh Kevod Shem Baruch) *[whispered]*←

This is the Genesis Prayer in its basic form. Each line has a specific meditation that you can either breeze through or take your time contemplating. It all depends on what you want to achieve and how much time you have. Before you begin, as with any meditation, you should sit down, relax, uncross your arms and legs, and think about what it is you want to accomplish with this meditation, and what's the spiritual component of that goal. In other words, if you achieve that goal, what aspect of sharing is there in it; how will society benefit; will it bring greater human dignity to the world; bring people together somehow? You don't want your goals to be of a selfish nature.

Of course, if you're standing on the street corner in the rain without an umbrella, you want to do the Genesis Prayer as quickly as possible, and while it might appear that your goal of getting a taxi instead of someone else is selfish, your real goal should be that everyone gets one, and/or that you want to get one in order to get home to do some act of sharing.

But assuming you do have time to meditate properly, you want to concentrate on making your goals unselfish ones. Let's say your goal is to close a huge business deal; by giving a portion of your earnings, tithing, to charity, your goal becomes spiritual. Think about it: if you couldn't close the deal without the Genesis Prayer, then you wouldn't have any of the earnings, so 90 percent is a lot better than nothing. But you shouldn't change your mind afterward, and decide it was your doing and not the will of the universe that made an unlikely deal happen for you; no one would be happy giving back that 100 percent. Of course, there are other ways to share than making a donation, like volunteering your time and/or your efforts to an altruistic cause.

Now let's say your goal is simpler and more immediate, like getting a taxi in the middle of a rainstorm when you're already standing on a street corner. You can't sit and meditate, so you do a quicker version of the Genesis Prayer, and put in the consciousness that you need to get home quicker so that you can help someone, maybe call someone who needs cheering up or something. Who should get that cab, the person in a hurry to do a selfless act of sharing, or the one thinking about how to screw a business partner?

~

HOW SETTING A GOAL CAN MAKE ALL THE DIFFERENCE

Paul, a film producer, was looking to take on a project that offered more than commercial reward. He wanted to do something that benefited people, not just enriched them. The opportunity came along not two days after Paul attended one of my Genesis Prayer seminars. And although there had been other opportunities in Paul's past, this time he was prepared to grab it. But from the start things didn't look promising. He was traveling up to meet the sponsors on what they'd said was "a very preliminary meeting," which were not encouraging words. Paul took them to mean that many people were being considered for the project. And even at the meeting, everyone reiterated that sentiment; the selection process had only just begun and Paul was only one of many being considered.

Paul felt he'd had a good meeting, but was nonetheless discouraged by their remarks. Still, he had a long drive home and in replaying the seminar in his head, he recalled that he could set a goal for himself at the outset of the Genesis Prayer and that the entire prayer would then work toward making it happen for him. So while driving home that's what he did, repeating the Genesis Prayer multiple times. He'd already told his wife about the futile trip, but just doing the Genesis Prayer made him feel better about it, and he shared his thoughts with her.

Then, one exit before returning home and minutes after reciting the final line of the prayer, his cell phone rang. It was the sponsors.

They'd started off by saying that they didn't really know why they were calling; after all, they'd just told him that they were weeks away from making any initial decisions. Nevertheless, they decided to forego the rest of the process and they hired Paul on the spot.

There were no other explanations. Paul didn't have any, and neither did his new sponsors. There's nothing as powerful as the Genesis Prayer to shift events and change destinies. There's nothing as quick. All we have to do is set our sights on an appropriate goal. Having a purpose in life makes it easier for the Genesis Prayer to help us realize it.

❧

In Part IV we list numerous meditations for each line, and I don't know of anyone who does them all, at least not at one sitting. They're included for you to pick and choose from as your life necessitates. The meditations have been resuscitated and compiled from the writings of many different sages, a few lines here, a few lines there. Most of the sages—Biblical, Talmudic, Kabalistic, and otherwise, spanning millennia—passed on their lessons verbally. Much of their writings are still hidden or have been destroyed, and many times they didn't bother to write down what they considered was already adequately covered by another sage. While they all used the basic Genesis Prayer extensively, we know from their writings that they concentrated on specific meditations and aspects of the prayer, ones that suited their individual needs. We've placed an asterisk before the most basic of the meditations and truthfully, that's all you need to see wondrous miracles in your life. So while the possible meditations are numerous, the basic ones can be reduced to one page, and we've done that for you in the summary section immediately following the line-by-line breakdown. In a pinch, simply scan the Hebrew/Aramaic line letters and ask for help. Enjoy the journey!

8

Activating the Meditations

IN THIS SECTION WE'RE GOING TO GO OVER THE GENESIS Prayer in a very basic and simple form without all the explanations and specialized meditations for things like finding your soul mate or getting help conceiving. These you'll find in Part IV, when we go over the Genesis Prayer in fine detail with the aim of drawing the most amount of energy and miracles into all areas of our lives.

Because we begin each line in the same way, with a specific invocation as to the energy source and type that we're going to tap into, we will explain the process using the first line as an example. For the rest of the lines we've highlighted the appropriate invocations and abbreviated the explanations, leaving the more involved explanations for Part IV.

LINE 1 *CHESED*
ALIGNING OURSELVES WITH THE UNIVERSE

When you're ready, you can say to yourself *"Chesed." Chesed* is pronounced *"hesed,"* with a strong "H." That signals to the universe from where you're drawing the energy. We know from the sages that *Chesed* is the level of mercy and is associated with Abraham, the Patriarch. Once you're familiar with these explanations and the

Genesis Prayer, you won't have to consciously think about any of this background information because it'll be embedded in your consciousness and your mind will automatically access it, just like driving to work without reviewing a map or the car's manual. So every time you do the Genesis Prayer and signal *Chesed* (חסד in Hebrew/Aramaic), you'll automatically be bringing mercy into your life.

The best way to draw in this energy, or the energy specific to any of the other seven lines is to request the support of the Patriarch whose energy corresponds to that particular line. In Hebrew/Aramaic, you'd say "*Chesed, Bizhoot Avraham Avinu,*" and in English you'd simply say, "Abraham, please help me," and the right energy will be there for you, helping you achieve your goals, in this case the energy of mercy/lovingkindness.

Next recite the first line two words at a time, from right to left:

Tsrurah Tatir   Yeminechah Gedulat   B'ko'ack Ana   ←

Again, by saying the words two at a time we're subliminally connecting to the right, left, and central columns and thus bringing balance into our lives without having to picture the columns or even think about them.

If you can read Hebrew or Aramaic, you can recite that text, but don't try to connect to the meaning of the words or you'll be limiting yourself.

אנא בכח גדולת ימינך תתירך צרור   (Chesed) חסד Line I ←

After reciting the first line, you should scan or at least glance at the six-letter Elevating Sequence at the end of the sentence (אבג יתצ). These are the first letters of each of the six words in the original Hebrew/Aramaic version; they are also the first six letters of the **42** letters that the meditation is based on. They are the code and the source of its miracle-giving properties. If we remember their names we recite them either out loud or to ourselves, but if not, we glance at them for the connection, lingering for a moment to complete the meditations that correspond to them:

צ ת י   ג ב א   (Elevating Sequence)

Tsaddie, Tav, Yud,   Gimmel, Bet, Alef   ←

The six letters above correspond to the six names of those letters below them, and if we want to we can pronounce them, but it's not really necessary. Following a tradition thousands of years old, we recite the lines in word pairs in order to subliminally process the energy in a balanced way, but we group the associated letters of the **42**-letter Name in triplets because each triplet forms its own balanced Name.

As we stated earlier, the letters represent the visible tips of enormous icebergs of energy, so to us they are simply symbols, whose shapes convey energy variations that we can't even comprehend. We can think of them as visual mantras or miniature meditation mandalas. It's like when a scientist sees the symbol for pi (π)—what he's thinking is $3.14159265358\ldots$—he's thinking about the energy behind this symbol that bends a straight line into a circle. When we see the letters of the meditation we don't have to think anything; we can concentrate instead on what the sages have told us about the energy of the line. That's why using the Genesis Prayer is so easy; we don't need to know any Hebrew or Aramaic whatsoever—all our connections are visual.

The sages—especially R. Hakana two thousand years ago and the later ones of the thirteenth, sixteenth, and eighteenth centuries, who were simply passing down the knowledge of sages who lived centuries and millennia earlier and whose penned tomes are now lost to the ages—have taught us many connections and secrets about the hidden codes in the Genesis Prayer, and there are many more yet to be revealed. Those secrets are based on combinations of the **42** letters as broken down line by line. Some of the letter combinations are based on the full six letters of the line, some on the two triplets that each line divides into, some on the three pairs that comprise each line's three columns, and some on a rearrangement (or permutation) of the letters as specified by the sages. For our purposes, we'll begin looking at each line the same way, by stating the associative energy level and its properties; the Patriarch who corresponds to that energy level; the six-word mantra of the line; and the six-letter meditative sequence. In Part IV, we'll list the individual meditative sequences of each line with their associated specific meditations and then go into a detailed description of each meditation, and how best to manifest that specific energy or property in our lives. In this section, we'll cover the basic and most important meditative connections that we all need to make so we can begin drawing miracles into our lives right away.

On the next page you'll begin your personal journey through the Genesis Prayer, shedding many illusions and much internal and external negativity along the way, all the while continually expanding your consciousness and aligning your soul with the energy of the universe and the Holy Spirit *(Ha'Shechinah)* or Divine Presence. As a result you will not only have a purer state of being, but a state in which you'll draw and see miracles in your life.

As you begin the first line, you should invoke its specific energy, *Chesed* or mercy/loving kindness, and its corresponding patriarch (Abraham), asking for his support. After you've read out loud the transliterated mantra that is that line, you want to begin the meditation by setting a goal for yourself, a lofty one, spiritual in nature, like getting a righteous child or soul mate, or even having a successful career, whereby you'll be able to share your wealth with others and with charitable causes. Once your goal is set, the subsequent meditations can begin working for you to achieve that goal. Have a wonderful journey!

LINE 1
Invocation: *Chesed*/Mercy—Loving Kindness/Abraham

(Recite two words at a time:)

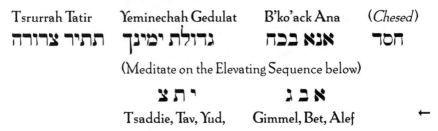

Tsrurrah Tatir	Yeminechah Gedulat	B'ko'ack Ana	(*Chesed*)	1
תתיר צרורה	גדולת ימינך	אנא בכח	חסד	1

(Meditate on the Elevating Sequence below)

י ת צ   א ב ג

Tsaddie, Tav, Yud,   Gimmel, Bet, Alef   ←

You should meditate on being one with the spiritual realm, letting the physicality around you vaporize as you connect to the Tree of Life reality, *Etz Ha'Cha'im,* the place of the ten dimensions where we have no limitations, and where we can reach our true potential and true fulfillment. This powerful elevating sequence begins with an invocation to "Our Father" (אב), and is the same value as the Hebrew/Aramaic phrase *"Ahavat kinam"* (unconditional love); therefore, we want to use it to imbibe from the supernal waters of unconditional love, meditating on the love we have for our children, parents, or pets and extending that love to everyone we know and on to the whole world, asking that all the senseless hatred in the world be replaced with human dignity. The more expansive our meditations, the bigger channel we'll be and the more miracles will flow into our lives.

When you're ready, go to the second line and say *"Gevurah,"* signaling to the universe that you're in the frame of *Gevurah* (pronounced giv-u-rah), the next level, which has the aspect of strength and proactivity.

LINE 2 *GEVURAH*
SHUTTING DOWN OUR REACTIVE NATURE, FREEING OUR SOUL

Invocation: *Gevurah*/Strength Against Temptation, and Removing Judgment/Isaac

(Recite two words at a time)

Jorah Taharenu	Sagvenu Amechah	Rinat Kahbel	(*Gevurah*)	2 ←
טהרנו נורא	עמך שגבנו	קבל רנת	(גבורה)	2 ←

(Meditate on the Proactive Sequence below)

ש ט נ   ק ר ע

Nun Tet Shin   Ayin Resh Koof   ←

In the first level we've opened the gates of certainty, and in this one we're cleansing away all the negative/destructive influences in our lives. Using this powerful proactive sequence, we can meditate to wrench out our evil inclination from the seed level; let go of all our doubts; shed our negativity, internal and external; and tear out our selfish and addictive desires from their roots. This letting go helps us to stop being reactive and start being proactive in everything we do, which in turn frees us from attracting judgment and lets us take control of our lives by attracting mercy instead.

As instructed in many books of the sages, we rearrange the letters to get *"sha'ar katan"* (שער קטן, small gate), and meditate to close these gates, the back doors where darkness and doubts slip in and interfere with our connections. Because we've opened a connection with the upper world, we want to keep it as pure as possible, and this line helps us do that.

This cleansing sequence is also the same value as the word *tishkack,* to forget. What we want to forget is the limitations we impose on ourselves by calculating and second-guessing our good intentions, which we do by letting our egos instead of the Light Force of God/Heaven do the thinking for us. When we're calculating, we're permitting others to control our destiny; we're allowing our fears to control it; we're succumbing to our doubts. We want to forget these limitations as well as the limitations of physicality, like time and space, so we can make room for miracles.

LINE 3 *TIFERET*
SUSTENANCE, HEALING, AND PROTECTION

Invocation: *Tiferet*/Beauty/Jacob

Shomrem Kevavat	Yichudechah Dorshay	Gibor Na	(*Tiferet*)	3
כבבת שמרם	דורשי יחודך	נא גבור	(תפארת)	3

(Meditate on the Protection Sequence below)

יכש   נגד

Shin Caf Yud   Dalet Gimmel Nun   ←

While meditating on this full six-letter sequence, we ask for protection of all sorts. Next, you should meditate on the first of the two powerful triplets from this line. All the triplets have their own special meditations, but we've highlighted only the ones that have been substantiated through multiple sources and have been proven by experience to be very effective.

נ ג ד   Dalet Gimmel Nun   ←

We meditate on this first triplet for sustenance through sharing and tithing, for forging a partnership with the Light of the Creator in everything we do. With the Light Force as our partner all blessings will flow to us, and there will be room in our lives for these blessings to enter.

י כ ש   Shin Caf Yud   ←

We meditate to use the second triplet as a spiritual *mikve*, or bath, for removing all our remaining negativity, and to go back in time and remove all the seeds of disease that we've accumulated in our lives since conception; removing all our emotional, psychological, physical, and spiritual scars; removing all our anger and jealousy. Once cleansed, we want to rejuvenate and replenish all those sparks of light that we've lost to the *klippot,* our dark side.

LINE 4 *NETZACH*
WILLPOWER AND BLESSINGS

Invocation: *Netzach*/Victory/Moses

▸mlem Tamid	Tsidkatechah Rackamay	Taharem Barckem	*Netzach*	4 ←
תמיד גמ◌	רחמי צדקתך	ברכם טהרם	(נצח)	4 ←

(Meditate on the Willpower Sequence below)

צ ת ג   ב ט ר

Gimmel Tav Tsaddie   Resh Tet Bet   ←

This sequence gives us the power of perseverance, the willpower to see things through to the end. It strengthens our resolve and infuses us with the Olympian spirit of going for and getting the gold. We can also use this sequence to strengthen our relationships, find our soul mates, and conceive children.

LINE 5 *HOD*
ENLIGHTENMENT

Invocation: *Hod*/Splendor/Aaron

▸atechah Nahel	Tuvchah Berov	Kadosh Khasin	*Hod*	5 ←
נהל עד◌	ברוב טובך	חסין קדוש	(הוד)	5 ←

(Meditate on the Enlightening Sequence below)

ט נ ע   ח ק ב

Ayin Nun Tet   Bet Koof Chet   ←

While meditating on this sequence, ask to receive the power of restriction—restriction from temptations that can lead you astray from a spiritual path and from your goals in life, especially the ones set forth at the onset of this prayer. Ask also to receive deep insight, clairvoyance *(ruach hakodesh)*, and the ability to read the signs all around you and to comprehend your dreams.

LINE 6 *YESOD*
DRAWING DOWN THE MIRACLES

Invocation: *Yesod*/Foundation/Yosef

K'dushatechah Zockray	P'nay L'amcha	Geh'eh Yackid	*Yesod*	6
זוכרי קדושתך	לעמך פנה	יחיד גאה	(יסוד)	6

(Meditate on the Expansion Sequence below)

פ ז ק   י ג ל

Koof Zayin Pay   Lamed Gimmel Yud   ←

Use this sequence to expand your consciousness. Begin by meditating on being One Soul with everyone in the world and then on spreading the wisdom of the Genesis Prayer to the far reaches of that soul, and in turn to the entire world. By doing this and by meditating to reveal the secrets of the sages and the Bible for everyone, you're expanding your personal vessel and making yourself the greatest possible channel for miracles to enter your life. Now meditate to usher in the Messiah *(Mashiach)* consciousness in this the sixth millennium of the Hebrew calendar, and you'll help bring it right into your life.

LINE 7 *MALCKUT*
MANIFESTING ALL THE MEDITATIONS

Invocation: *Malckut*/Kingdom/Manifestation/
King David and the Messiah

'alumot Yode'ah	Tsa'akatenu Ushma	Kahbel Shavatenu	*Malckut*	7 ←
יודע תעלומו	ושמע צעקתנו	שועתנו קבל	(מלכות)	7 ←

(Meditate on the Manifestation Sequence)

צ י ת   ש ק ו

Tav Yud Tsaddie   Vav Koof Shin   ←

Meditate to renew and refresh all your relationships, including the one with the creative forces of the universe, this time with the powerful help of the Genesis Prayer. This meditation will help to undo any mistakes we've made in our lives, especially with the people we care about as well as those we work with in our daily lives.

As we meditate on these six letters we want to think again about that lofty goal we set for ourselves and about what we want to achieve in life, because this is the level where all the connections we've made get manifested. Rethink anything that you can remove or change in your way of being that might get in the way of that manifestation, and this line will help you achieve it.

Next, whisper this final phrase silently to yourself in order to ground the connections and to help build your vessel to receive all the blessings derived from the prayer above.

(ועד	מלכותו לעולם	ברוך שם כבוד)	
(Va'ed	L'olam Malckhutoh	Kevod Shem Baruch)	← (whisper silently)

PART IV

THE GENESIS PRAYER

MASTER MEDITATION

9

Line 1—Unconditional Love

CHESED/MERCY AND LOVINGKINDNESS/ABRAHAM (MANTRA)

rurah Tatir	Yeminechah,Gedulat	B'ko'ack Ana	(*Chesed*)	1 ←
תתיר צרור	גדולת ימינך	אנא בכח	(חסד)	1 ←
	י ת צ	א ב ג		
	Tsaddie, Tav, Yud,	Gimmel, Bet, Alef		←

The first step in our meditative process is to set a lofty spiritual goal—all the rest of the meditations will act on your behalf to achieve that goal as speedily as possible, each building on the next to remove the obstacles in your way. We should whisper to ourselves what we want to get out of the prayer, out of life, and we should phrase this goal as a forgone conclusion, as if we've already achieved it. For example, if you want to meet your soul mate, picture yourself already married to him or her, and state: I'm married to my soul mate and we're doing our spiritual work. Whatever you wish for, add the words "to do my spiritual work."

The summary of meditative sequences provided below is explained in detail in the subsequent pages. In each case, the letters are what we concentrate on and the parenthetical instructions are what we should think about. The asterisks indicate that the corresponding sequence is more critical; the other meditative sequences are optional.

Summary Meditations

The asterisks indicate the most important ones

אבג יתצ	Our Father
	(Connect to Abraham, to the Father of spirituality, and to Our Father in Heaven)
אבג יתצ	Tapping into the Whole 5 Books
	(Connect to and wrap yourself in the energy of the entire Pentateuch [Torah])
אבג יתצ	*Unconditional Love
	(Meditate on feeling and sharing unconditional love for the whole world)
אנא	The Power of Cleansing
	(Meditate on bathing and cleansing yourself inside and out with spiritual water or Light)
אבג יתצ	*In Heaven/Tree of Life Reality
	(Dissolve the world around you until you find yourself in the spiritual realm, where there are no limitations)

OUR FATHER

Connect to Abraham, to the Father of Spirituality, and to Our Father in Heaven

Is it a coincidence that this prayer begins with the letters *Alef Bet*?

אבג יתצ

These two letters are the first two of the Hebrew alphabet, equivalent to "A" and "B." They are also the first two of the name

Abraham. And they also spell out the word *Av,* father, *Abba,* in Aramaic, leaving little doubt as to the prayer's intentions. In Jewish and old Christian prayers, *Abba* was a Name by which God was addressed. It later became a title for bishops, and even the word *abbot* is a derivation of *Abba.* Indeed, the name starts off the best-known prayer of all time, Our Father, or the Lord's Prayer.

The sages tell us that "Father" at the commencement of the Genesis Prayer is a reference to our primordial thought process, much as a father is the source of the seed in the creation process. This placement of "father" (אב) inspires our highest thoughts, while the journey through the next forty words/letters and seven lines strengthens our aspirations and brings them to fruition.

To my two-year-old son, the 1, 2, and 3 status of the letters in the first sequence (אבג) is akin to "On your mark, get set, go," but to the sages, it represents the three highest levels closest to God, and their sum, six, reflects the six lower ones, an analogy of the process through which the Light of God is channeled down to us at the tenth (the earthly or physical) level, represented by the Yud (י) of the subsequent sequence (יתץ), and thus this simple sequence is a bridge to God and heaven and, as we'll explain shortly, to what the Pentateuch describes as the "Tree of Life" reality. It's no wonder that this first six-letter sequence is the most important of the entire Genesis Prayer, and the most powerful.

My wife recently reminded me of a couple in Toronto who became nervous because the only line of the Genesis Prayer they could remember was the first line. They had recently learned the Genesis Prayer, and as they were walking home late one Friday evening, they realized someone was following them, someone they didn't know, someone big. The streets were dark. They were at least three long blocks from home, and taking a side street would have only made their predicament worse. Most of the lights in the homes were out, save a few sporadic courtesy lights above the porches, and none nearby. When they checked over their shoulders again to make sure he wasn't some figment of their imagination, he'd gotten closer. He was speeding up. They, too, quickened their pace, afraid to break out into an all-out run lest he'd realize their panic. He sped up as well. Owen could feel his wife's hand clutching his, her nails digging into his wrist. He could also feel his heart pounding against the wall of his chest. Despite his own distress, he could see the trouble his wife was having keeping up with him in her high heels.

A million thoughts raced through his head. Should he turn and confront this guy, who was half again larger than he? Knowing he had to defend his wife somehow, Owen gripped down on the keys in his pocket, slipping each through the fingers in his clenched fist. They'd be his weapon of last resort, but would be little consolation against a knife or gun. The guy was less than thirty feet away, and his rapid steps echoed as they slapped heavily on the pavement. Owen tried to remember the Genesis Prayer, but in all the confusion, only the first line came out. His wife, too, could only recall the first line, and they recited it together, half in silence, completely in panic: *Ana B'ko'ack, Gedulat Yeminechah, Tatir Tsrurah.*

Owen turned to face their pursuer, but he was now more than fifty feet back and slowing considerably. Owen and his wife, with hearts pounding and labored breath, slowed a little, too, but the stranger slowed more. Frequent glances over their shoulders showed him to be half a block, then a full block behind them. Then he disappeared entirely and they soon arrived at their home safe and sound, mystified, but thankful.

The power in this line is what saved Owen and his wife. The power in this line is why the sages tell us that if we're ever in danger or in an emergency, we should meditate and recite this line.

We should also seek help when possible. The powerful first line of the Genesis Prayer worked for Owen and his wife and for countless others, but we should never rely solely on our spiritual tools, for we never know the true depth of our certainty of them or the full extent of the danger we may be in. These tools are gifts to make things easier for us, not to do all the work for us. We can think of them as power screwdrivers; we still have to hold them and place the screw in the right place. The Genesis Prayer is more like a power drill or even a jackhammer, but we still have to direct the power consciously. We must participate and do our best in whatever situation we find ourselves in.

TAPPING INTO
THE WHOLE 5 BOOKS AT ONCE

Connect to and Wrap Yourself in the Energy of the Entire Pentateuch (Torah)

The collective numerical value of the first line or first 6 letters of the Genesis Prayer is 506. That was simple arithmetic, and the corresponding meditation taught to me by my teacher was powerful, but what we learned next floored me. I'd already known the power of the Genesis Prayer, but I had no idea to what extent it was integrated into the Pentateuch (Torah), or how much high-powered space-age technology went into designing both of them. As stated earlier, there are fourteen triplets that comprise the forty-two letters of the prayer. These fourteen triplets occur naturally somewhere in the Pentateuch, either within words, or simply as a sequence of letters ending one word and beginning another. That's to be expected, given that there are 304,805 letters in the Pentateuch, but what's astonishing is that if we add up all the times that each of those fourteen triplets occurred, we'd get exactly 506 times. Given that there are over 300,000 different triplets in the Torah, the odds against this being a chance occurrence are astronomical.

It's amazing: by designing the Genesis Prayer thus, the fourteen triplets draw upon the entire energy of the Pentateuch and put it *all* at our disposable. It would take all night for a fast and skilled reader to read the entire Pentateuch in its original Hebrew, whereas we, without knowing any Hebrew, can tap into all its power and glory and focus it right into the areas of our lives where we need it the most, all in just a few minutes, all by just reciting the first line if need be. Though it can't be proven yet, the Pentateuch (Torah) is supposed to have been dictated by God to Moses, who dictated it to the Israelites. It can't be proven that He didn't, either.

Indeed, with so many astonishing mathematically impossible coincidences designed into the Torah, it's difficult to see how it could be man-made. Regardless who we believe created the Torah, the sages have shown in innumerable books that the Torah is both a channel and generator of divine energy and that it is rife with powerfully charged encrypted connections, many of which we'll be illustrating in this book.

UNCONDITIONAL LOVE

Meditate on Feeling and Sharing Unconditional Love for the Whole World

The most important message of all built into the Genesis Prayer is love, the unconditional love that a father has for his child. That's why that love is built into the first line, the line connected to Abraham and "father." It represents the unconditional, all-encompassing love a young child has for his father. As we've just said, the sages tell us that these first six letters add up numerically to the value 506, which is the value of the Hebrew/Aramaic phrase *ahavat kinam,* unconditional love, and that the central two letters of this line have the numerical value of 13, that same as *ahava,* the word "love," itself. Therefore, they go on to explain, as we begin the Genesis Prayer we should be meditating on loving our neighbors as ourselves, a phrase also numerically encoded into this first line.

This line and its energy connect us to the tears Abraham shed when he held the knife to sacrifice his beloved son Isaac. It also invokes the love Abraham had for the Lord and the certainty he had in the Lord that brought him to the point of sacrificing his son. The sages tell us God never intended Abraham to slay his son and that He never had any doubts as to Abraham's fulfilling the strange request, but that Abraham's fellow man needed to see what true devotion and love were all about. On one of the many levels of understanding built into the Pentateuch (Torah), Abraham's actions are an example or blueprint for us, and on another level, his story is providing us with an interface that we can tap into and that absorbs some of that love and certainty. The Genesis Prayer, as always, acts as a bridge to the Torah, and to the source of that love.

יתצ   **אבג**

Tsaddie, Tav, Yud,   Gimmel, Bet, Alef   ←

Because unconditional love is an abstraction and hard to contemplate, an easier way to tap into the feeling is to think about loving your neighbors as you do your children if you have any. If not, as you love(d) your parents, or as you love(d) a pet. Regardless, find someone or something to which you have an emotional loving attachment and try to visualize transferring those feelings to the people you know around you, then to strangers in your vicinity, and then to the guy who bumped into you and didn't apologize, or some such incident. When you can no longer think of him as a jerk, you're tapping into unconditional love.

Like the butterfly beating its wings in China, your actions are having a quantum effect on the entire planet. Yes, just by doing this simple meditation, you're helping to shift the consciousness of society and saving lives somewhere around the world. That's why the universe will pay you back with a miracle. We scratch its back; it scratches ours.

BREAKING THE CODE

We know from the sages that the complimentary technology embedded in both the Genesis Prayer and the Bible's first verse is endless, and as will be explained in Part VI. This first line (יתצ אבג) can be translated numerically to 123149, which, as we'll see, literally spells out the powerful Creation Equation that's cryptically embedded in the Bible's first verse. But what's significant for us in our meditations concerning this first line is that **314** is doubly representative of the specific Name of God, *Shaddai* (שׁדי), the Almighty—the Name on every *mezuzah*—and as the sages explain, when *Shaddai* is spelled out, its numerical value is that of the famous Biblical phrase from Leviticus 19:18, "And you shall love your neighbor as yourself," which is the whole essence of unconditional love and of the Genesis Prayer. According to the second-century *Zohar (Book of Splendor)*, the first-century B.C.E. sage Hillel the Elder, and several books of the New Testament, this is the fundamental purpose of the Torah: to forgo our selfish desires and to get us to love our neighbors as ourselves. By cryptically embedding this connection into the Genesis Prayer's first line, we've been given a way to tap into this unconditional loving energy.

~~

THE POWER OF CLEANSING

Meditate on Bathing and Cleansing Yourself Inside and Out with Spiritual Water or Light

There is another coded blessing built into the Genesis Prayer, and it's built right into the first word of the first line in two different ways:

Line 1 חסד (Chesed) אנא בכח גדולת ימינך תתיר צרורה

When we use one of those ancient code-breaking ciphers called small *gematria* to translate the letters in the word *Ana* (אנא), into their numerical equivalents, they spell out 1-5-1, or 151, which is the value of the Hebrew/Aramaic word *mikve*, a special cleansing bath that Abraham instructed all his guests to take. According to the sages, there's nothing more powerful than a *mikve* to cleanse away our accumulated negativity, because there's nothing more powerful than life-sustaining water for cleansing. And it must be important, because the value 151 is one of the very few core numbers that the Pentateuch (Torah) is built around. Just the fact that the name Abraham is found 151 times in the Pentateuch is proof enough of how important it is to the Pentateuch, to Abraham, and to the line of the Genesis Prayer intimately connected to the energy of Abraham.

~

BREAKING THE CODE

According to the ancient sages, the number **151** also represents two of the most powerful names of God used in the Pentateuch, both of them in their expanded spelled-out forms. One is *Ehyeh* (אהיה), whose sum of the spelled-out (*gematria milui*) letters (אלף הה יוד הה') is numerically equivalent to 151, and the other is the expanded spelled-out small *gematria* version of the Tetragrammaton (יהו'ה) inclusive of all four of its levels (יוד הי ויו 'הי+יוד הי ואו 'הי+יוד הא ואו 'הא+יוד הה וו 'הה).

~

The second way the word *mikve* is coded into the beginning of the Genesis Prayer is deciphered by examining the first three letters (אקנ) of the first vertical column of the prayer. Once again the letters spell out the value 151—this time using the most basic of the *gematria* ciphers.

		↓
יתצ	אבג	
שׁטנ	קרע	
יכשׁ	נגד	
צתג	בטר	
טנע	חקב	
פזק	יגל	
צית	שׁקו	

But what all this means for *us* are pure blessings. Just as we begin the Genesis Prayer, it's as if we're being immersed in a powerful *mikve,* Abraham's *mikve,* and being purged and cleansed of a tremendous amount of accumulated negativity. It's as if thick shells or multiple layers of husks were being removed from our being in order to let in the light. Not only that, but at the same time we're being embraced by and wrapped in the energy of the Lord. As we continue doing the Genesis Prayer, that bathing, cleansing, embracing, and wrapping process continues, protecting us and protecting our meditations from any negativity that might try to slip into our consciousness. It's interesting that the first three lines are blanketed by that protective power because they're the most powerful ones, and as we've seen, the last two lines get special energy boosts to compensate and help the energy to flow freely.

The beauty in this technology is incredible! The beauty in these **42** letters and all that they offer us is mind-boggling, and it's all here for us without us even having to think about it! Once we know it's there and we've unconsciously absorbed it into our minds, it'll be there for us to tap into whenever we like.

SPIRITUAL CLEANSING IN THE REAL WORLD

Stress and chaos not only are caused by negativity, but perpetuate it, and as a preschool in Manhattan found out, a simple cleansing tool like the Genesis Prayer can wipe all that stress and chaos away in an instant. Eunice is the head teacher at a prestigious Manhattan preschool, but still she seemed to be in over her head when the school directors decided to convert the school to a summer day camp on short notice. With all the other teachers on summer vacation, Eunice was forced to make do with an untested staff of teenagers and volunteers in a program she'd never managed before. Making matters worse, the camp ranks were swelling with the directors' children in for the summer and the children of assorted celebrities who were persuaded to sign up. With a week to go before they were to officially open with thirty campers ages two through six, they did a dry run with only nine children and as Eunice feared, it was a disaster. Nothing went right, nothing. At the end of the week everyone wanted to quit.

Opening day, July 6, began differently. Before the parents of the thirty little campers could drop off their kids, backpacks and all, Eunice and her staff were led through a complete Genesis Prayer.

Talk about miracles! Everything went supersmooth. *(Bli ayn hara.)*

The parents said their good-byes without scenes, the counselors did their jobs with smiles and élan, and the kids had a great time: no fights, no miscues, not the smallest commotion. Remember, we're talking about two-year-olds and untrained teenagers. Even the children who were known to be troublesome were well behaved. No one could believe the change. The staff, which only a few days earlier refused to cooperate and help clean up, were picking up after each other as they went. Everyone said the energy of the place got lighter and was cheerier. Needless to say, they made the Genesis Prayer part of their morning routine and had a wonderful summer. *(Bli ayn hara.)*

We cannot underestimate the power of injecting unconditional love into a place or situation no matter what the circumstances. It changes everything.

IN HEAVEN/TREE OF LIFE REALITY

Dissolve the World Around You Until You Find Yourself in the Spiritual Realm, Where There Are No Limitations

Once we've meditated on unconditional love and bathed in that warm energy, we want to meditate on what we're connecting to, the "Tree of Life reality" *(Etz Ha'Chayim)*, which refers to the Tree of Life in the middle of the Garden of Eden in Genesis. The Tree of Life is really a code word for the reality beyond our five senses, a reality where the parallel universes coexist and we can be in any one of them we chose. It's a place where, as in the story of Adam and Eve, anything and everything is available to us at our whim. Think of the Tree of Life as an elevator to a higher dimension, to a spiritual place where all things are possible, to heaven. Our leading scientists tell us the other dimensions exist, and the sages insisted on it, so we might as well do as the sages did.

For the sages, who were at a much higher level spiritually than us, this was probably the most important connection—their instant elevator to the spirit world. The Tree of Life reality is a reality whereby we can shift up and down the scale of dimensions at will and with each one expand our consciousness and the speed with which we can access information, thus empowering us to shift the events around us. We can't do that on our own, but we don't have to. We can do it the way the sages did—using the Genesis Prayer. All we need is the right state of consciousness, telling ourselves we want to tap into the Tree of Life *(Etz Ha'Chayim)* reality, and that we want to dematerialize all the illusions and limitations of this world. The code word Tree of Life is given to us in Genesis[3], knowing it is like having the secret password that lets us through the gate to a new reality.

~

BREAKING THE CODE

It sounds like modern science fiction or even cutting-edge physics, but once properly translated, Abraham's four thousand-year-old *Sefer Yetzirah* and the second-century *Zohar* both explain this shifting of events in concrete scientific terms. In fact, Richard Feymann's multiple history scenario describes something very similar.

---

[3] The Tree of Life is in the fortieth verse of Genesis, forty always being a marker for biblical "coming of age," prophecy, and special blessings.

Imagine our physical lives and world stretched out from the beginning of history to the end. This is called *our* plane of existence. Now picture it smack in the middle of all those parallel universes, those parallel planes of existence, in which the exact same thing is going on in each universe, just going on a fraction of a second before the next. If you were only one dimension higher up on the Tree, which would be the fifth dimension, you'd be able to traverse time without creating a causality violation, in other words, without violating the modern philosophical conundrum, the Grandfather Paradox, the one that says you can't go back in time because you might create a chain of events that cause you not to be born in the first place, such as killing your grandfather or causing him not to marry your grandmother.

Just by shifting universes, you could move anywhere in the future or past, like a needle skipping along the grooves of an LP record, setting down wherever you choose.

Then, if you were to move up to the next or sixth dimension, where all the universes would be mutations or variations of that original parallel universe, you'd be able to access anything you wanted instantly, anywhere, any place, any time. Just imagine the seventh dimension, where you'd find even time itself mutated. We can't. But we don't have to; the Genesis Prayer accesses it for us.

Typically, when I demonstrate the Genesis Prayer in our seminars I have everyone visualize the room and everything in it fading away. When you do that, your consciousness shifts and you feel as if you're floating in the endless realm with no limitations, where everything is only a thought away.

It's an amazing experience, but the truth is we couldn't possibly visualize that limitless spiritual realm if we wanted to, because even our thoughts can't exist there—they're too slow. This is why when we do the Genesis Prayer, objects and people pop in and out of our reality, things that weren't there a moment before, or things we may not have even asked for. Allison asked for her train to go faster, not for it to be detoured. Carmela asked for her taxi to get through traffic, not for her daughter's safety. The universe is ready for us; our thoughts are so far behind they're off the radar screen. Simply by acknowledging our limitations and saying we want to enter the Tree of Life reality we're expanding our consciousness and allowing the Genesis Prayer to take us there.

When we say to ourselves we're dissolving our reality and supplanting it with the Tree of Life reality, we're also telling ourselves that we're suspending the illusions of time, space, and motion, which are the illusions that keep us wedded to physicality, to the physical world, and that hold us back from reaching our true potentials.

The way the word *life* in the Tree of Life is spelled in Genesis includes an extra *hey* (ה) as a seemingly unnecessary prefix, but that addition changes everything; it is what gives the power to the phrase. The value of the word *life* becomes 73 instead of 68, which seems trivial, but as we'll see in Part VI, the value 73 connects the phrase to creation itself and is the irremovable link between it, the Genesis Prayer, and the formation of the universe at its most fundamental level.

Don't worry, you don't have to remember this esoteric material. The important meditations will be repeated in the summary section. You'll see firsthand that this entire first line with all its relevant meditations will take you all of twenty seconds.

10

Line 2—Shutting Down Our Reactive Nature

GEVURAH/STRENGTH AND JUDGMENT/ISAAC

ɔrah Taharenu	Sagvenu Amechah	Rinat,Kahbel	(*Gevurah*)	1 ←
טהרנו נו	עמך שגבנו	קבל רנת	(גבורה)	2 ←
	שׁ ט נ	ק ר ע		
	Nun Tet Shin	Ayin Resh Koof	←	

Ask that Isaac, the Patriarch, add strength and support to all your connections. When we say this to ourselves, we're actively connecting to a specific type of energy and also helping to complete a cosmic puzzle, a rectification of the unity that existed prior to the Big Bang. Each line, each Patriarch, is a symbol of a specific type of energy, one that has its own special frequency that resonates especially well with the letters of its associated line. By drawing upon the appropriate energy line by line, we not only can balance the energy of our lives, but we can connect part and parcel to the cosmic wholeness and divine unity of the greater universe. The sages have written volumes explaining the nature of this energy, but they tell us that all we have to do to activate it is to say aloud, or even to whisper to ourselves, "*Gevurah,* may the merit of

Isaac, the Patriarch, help us." Or in Hebrew/Aramaic, *"Gevurah, Bizhoot Yitzchak Avinu."*

Summary of Meditative Sequences

קרע שטנ	Deliver Us from Evil, Our Own Negativity (Meditate to cut out your negative inclinations)
קרע שטנ	Building the Desire to Share (Let go of your selfish desires)
שער קמנ	Closing the Small Gates/Stop Being Reactive (Meditate to not be influenced by the negativity of others, and ask for strength against their provocations)
קרע שטנ	As We Forgive Others/Being Proactive (Ask for the strength to get out of your comfort zone and to go the extra mile)
קרע and שטנ	Reducing Our Ego and Personal Agendas (Meditate to take your ego and personal agendas out of your dealings, and to stop calculating and second- guessing your good intentions)
קרע שטנ	Letting Go of Our Doubts (Suspend your disbelief and go with the flow. Meditate to keep the gates of certainty open.)
קרע שטנ	Moving Heaven and Earth (Meditate on a specific situation you want changed and what outcome you'd like to see)

DELIVER US FROM EVIL, OUR OWN NEGATIVITY

Meditate to Cut Out Your Negative Inclinations

This line (קרע שטנ) forms a phrase, *kara Satan,* which literally means "to tear out Satan," but Satan to the sages isn't some red guy with a tail and horns; it's a code word for our own evil inclination, our negative inclination, our selfish desires, the things we know are wrong or bad for us yet we do anyway, the things we demand because of our egos. The word *satan* originally meant adversary, and referred to the personal adversary we all have inside us that advises us against doing the right thing. This sequence helps us to reduce those desires, thus increasing our desire to share with others and helping to keep us on the right track. The sages also point out another sequence (עקר שׂטנ), *akar Satan,* which means "to pull out Satan," an even more emphatic version of the meditation/message above, because it helps us pull the negativity out by its roots. They recommend saying both of them: *kara Satan* and *akar Satan.*

BUILDING THE DESIRE TO SHARE

Let Go of Your Selfish Desires

Think of our essential being, our spiritual vessel, so to speak, as a cup filled with water and oil, the water representing our desire to share and the oil our negative inclination or selfish desires. The cup can only hold so much, and as you know, the oil or negativity floats on top, giving the world the false impression that that's all we are. But if we add more water, more aspects of sharing, the water will rise and the oil will spill off the top, allowing the world to eventually see the beauty in our true nature. Appropriately enough, water is considered *Chesed,* mercy, because it always wants to share, with everything but oil, with which it can't mix. We can use this second line of the Genesis Prayer to draw down the energy of sharing from the first line, *chesed*/mercy/lovingkindness, by meditating on קרע שׂטנ and letting it tear away at our negativity, letting it automatically root it out at the seed level—at its fundamental source—and thus filling our hearts and minds with the ability and urge to share. The sages refer to it as the seed level, because a seed contains the DNA blueprint for the entire tree and even its subsequent generations. So when we alter something at the seed level, we're changing everything that follows.

CLOSING THE SMALL GATES/
STOP BEING REACTIVE

Meditate to Not Be Influenced by the Negativity of Others, and Ask for Strength Against Their Provocations

When we follow the sages' instructions and rearrange the letters in קרע שטן, we get the phrase *sha'ar katan* (שער קטן), which means "small gate." This line helps us to close these small gates, and not let in our darker desires. It's the small gates we have to worry about, and the Pentateuch instructs us to put policemen and judges at our gates, which according to the sages means for us to post guards at our mouths, ears, and eyes, because we can't trust our senses, and because when we slip and judge others, we're really rendering judgment upon ourselves. This line helps us remove some of the judgments issued against us, judgments caused by our own negative inclination. The sages also tell us this line connects us to the level of *Gevurah,* which is associated with strength, but even more often with judgment.

The universe can use either judgment or mercy to wake us up and to teach us spiritual lessons. In the biblical sense judgment is divine retribution, a form of punishment for our transgressions, karmic payback, and something we'd like to avoid at all costs. By executing this sequence we're telling the universe that we are awake, that we're listening, and that we'd rather learn through mercy.

The sages also tell us that in order to keep from incurring more judgment, we should watch what we say, because words can't be taken back and gossip is like germs in the wind; watch what we see, because the eyes are our windows to the soul and they absorb everything into our consciousness; watch what we listen to, because by enabling gossip and evil speech we're just as guilty as he who spoke it. Because none of us are saints, we have the Genesis Prayer to cleanse away much of our accumulated, although inadvertent, negativity. The sages further explain that we should be vigilant against the small things that can trip us up because a small hole in the dike eventually leads to a huge flood, and that this sequence helps us to close off those holes in our character.

What we want to do is put strong judges at our gates and not let the darkness into our lives in the first place, and the best way to do that is to shut down our reactive system, that is, the force within us that always has to be right, that has to have an answer for everything, that gets insulted and upset when we hear something with which we don't agree—all the things that create separation from our fellow man.

BREAKING THE CODE

The value of the word *judge* is also encoded into the line using the hyperrevelatory small *gematria* cipher. With it, the triplet שׁמב has the value 395, that of the word *judge*. It's clues such as these, along with divine inspiration, that allowed the sages to determine the usage for each line, and then, once they were in an elevated state, they could see for themselves if they were correct.

AS WE FORGIVE OTHERS/BEING PROACTIVE

Ask for the Strength to Get Out of Your Comfort Zone and to Go the Extra Mile

When someone bothers us, we should stop and think before we react; we should do something against our nature, against our instincts; we should do something proactive. If you do this, amazingly, the situation will defuse and whatever it is that was bothering you will disappear. As successful as this proactive formula is, it works even better if we're proactive in everything we do. There's a highly successful accounting firm whose senior partners have a pact that they'll tackle their hardest problem of the day first: the call they least want to make, the client they least want to face, or the mistake they least want to own up to. They've learned that if they procrastinate and don't tackle the issue first thing in the morning and get it out of the way, it will fester and get worse, and it'll be on their minds all day long, interfering with all their other business and decisions. That's being proactive. With the hardest task of the day out of the way, the rest of the day is easy. That's logical. It's also spiritual, because it's a result of the partners having been proactive, going against their nature and not giving in to their negative inclination, the voice in the back of our heads whispering to us to put off confrontation, to put off doing the tasks, that everything will work out by itself.

We can shut down that voice, but only by going against our nature, by not being reactive, and in turn by being proactive. When that voice tell us "just one more drink, what'll it hurt," or "go ahead and have that dessert; it's just a small piece," or even "I'm tired, I'll get back to her later," that's when we need go against our nature and not give in, proactively restricting before it's too late.

This second line of the Genesis Prayer gives us the strength to be proactive.

REDUCING OUR EGO AND PERSONAL AGENDAS

Meditate to Take Your Ego and Personal Agendas Out of Your Dealings, and to Stop Calculating and Second-Guessing Your Good Intentions

The small *gematria* of the triplet (שטב) also has the same value as "the heavens" or just plain "heaven," and (קרע) has the value of "your heaven," thus allowing us to draw on that special energy as we overcome all that causes us to be reactive in the first place, which, in reality, is our ego. If we didn't have ego or could control it, we wouldn't be bothered by the actions of others, we couldn't get insulted, and our feelings wouldn't be hurt. We often get upset because we have personal agendas, even behind seemingly altruistic actions. We're not giving advice for the sake of sharing, we're really giving it because we want to get out our pet theories, because we want the other person to go through what we did, or because we want them to like us more or to owe us something. When we give advice like that, there's no way it'll work out well, not for the other person nor for us. It always backfires. We need to remove our egos and personal agendas, and let the Light of inspiration flow directly through us.

The Hebrew/Aramaic word for "to forget," *tishkack,* has the same numerical value as both triplets together, and to activate the strengths of this line we should meditate that we want to forget all our limitations, especially the limitations we impose on ourselves. Often, in life, we get the flash of a good idea or think of a positive deed that we can do; when we follow through we are being proactive and the sages tell us that the outcome from such an action has to be good. More often than not, instead of taking that course of action, we make calculations in our heads: "If I do it, he'll do this," or "What if it's not the right decision," and so on. When we calculate the outcome, we limit ourselves.

Of course, weighing the results of our actions is human nature, but it's also the nature we want to overcome. We don't want to let the chips fall where they may, we want to take control of our lives and rise above our nature. We want to forget these limitations, which are only our egos speaking. Only our ego would say to the universe that we know better. Our egos are only motivated by selfish desires. What we want to forget are the illusions of our negative inclination. We want to choose the strength of Heaven to steer us on the right path, and forget the limitations of our five senses.

When we're calculating, we're not being proactive; we're being reactive. We're letting others control our destiny; we're letting our fears control it; we're succumbing to our doubts. When you've been given the gift of a positive idea, never calculate, never hesitate, just do it. Responding quickly and decisively is the only way you can be sure the outcome is what the universe wanted for you and how you can be sure you're getting what's best for you. How often have you gotten the answers to your prayers, but second-guessed them? If you're like me, it probably happened so often you've lost track. Whom do we have to blame for things not working out the way we wanted? Only ourselves. This second line of the Genesis Prayer gives us the strength to overcome our second-guessing, to overcome our nature.

LETTING GO OF OUR DOUBTS

Suspend Your Disbelief and Go with the Flow. Meditate to Keep the Gates of Certainty Open.

קרע שטן

I've learned a lot through my teachers and my investigations, but the most important lesson I've learned is that I don't have all the answers. So instead of asking "Why?" all the time, I've trained my-self to ask "Why not?," which wasn't easy. I come from a scientific, right-mind, logic-oriented background and my nature is to question everything, but there came a point when I had to say "enough." I'd already seen a preponderance of evidence and digging any further for the sake of gnosis, the pure pursuit of knowledge, was self-defeating; it was taking me further away from the true revelations. It was only when I started asking "Why not?" Instead of "Why?" that I felt connected; it was only then that I started getting real an-swers and could grasp the significance and importance of the Gen-esis Prayer. Yes, the Light of the Creator is beneficent and gave me miracles *(Bli ayn hara)* all along the way, but it was only when I could say, "It's not me, it's the Light" that things truly opened up for me. Happiness is elusive, and the more we search for it the more elusive it gets. If we stop long enough to let in the Light, it'll find us. The Genesis Prayer will tell the Light where to find us, but we can't make ourselves a moving target. Just shrug your shoulder and say, "Why not?" then go with it. Take it from me, don't fight the process, *let go*.

What we want to forget most of all are our doubts, which are the biggest limitation of all. Doubts are another form of ego, perhaps the worst kind and certainly the most pervasive. The only reason we don't have total and complete certainty in the power of the Light of the Creator is that we feel that maybe we know better. We can acknowledge that the laws of the universe work, and if only I'd do the Genesis Prayer with the right consciousness I know I'd get miracles, but maybe, just maybe, I can do it on my own without miracles. Perhaps I won't want what the universe wants to give me, so I'll go after what I'm more comfortable with. All the maybes are simply indications that we think we can do it better. It is a shame, because if we'd only shove aside our doubts and keep the gates of certainty propped open, everything we could ever ask for would flow our way. We want to wrench out the doubts from inside us, digging all the way down to the roots. We don't want to let doubts through the small gates. You could walk away from reading this book, all pumped up and ready to do an amazing Genesis Prayer and bring a great miracle into your life, maybe a soul mate, maybe a child, but you mention the prayer to a relative or a friend who's got a personal agenda—they all have them, we all do—and someone who's never tried it themselves tells you they have some inside info into this ancient technology or knows something even better, and the next thing you know, you've fallen, you've let the doubts in through the smallest of gates. Now, instead of your miracle, you're stuck once again in the muck of negativity and agendas, you're stuck within the chaos, stress, and strife that everyone else calls life, everyone who hasn't received this gift and seen for themselves that there's a better way—the way it was always meant to be.

Certainty is the key. This book will give you all the ammunition you need to have certainty in the Light of the Creator, and if you can keep it, all the tools and blessings in the Genesis Prayer and life will be activated for you. Don't let those doubts back in, but if they do return, meditate to remove them while doing this second line—that's the reason it's there.

There's a story that comes to mind. It's about an intrepid adventurer who was out mountain climbing alone one winter day. He was making great progress even as the clouds rolled in, and as high up as he was, that meant a cold snowy fog. Still, he was near his goal and decided to push on. Then he slipped, his ice pick snagging loose snow. Losing his balance, he tumbled backward and downward, but only a short way. Fortunately, the last piton he'd placed held and though he was dangling above a huge precipice he could regain his composure and footing, though now he'd have to climb up by a different route, one with which he wasn't familiar. As the clouds thickened, trouble returned and this time when he fell, the pitons didn't hold, they pulled out slowly at first, one at a time, until they popped like machine-gun fire and he free-fell, bouncing off one icy wall to the next, dropping, screaming, into oblivion.

Finally his ropes snagged and held, but he was left dangling in the fog, somewhere off the side of the mountain. Everything all around him was white, and his own head was a white daze itself.

Eventually he composed himself and tried shouting for help, though he knew it was to no avail—no one would hear him, and even if someone did, they'd never find him. He himself couldn't see more than two feet in front of his face. Time passed; how long, he couldn't tell—he'd lost track in his exhaustive struggle against the cold and the elements to find secure footing and climb back up. After a long time, he decided to make his peace. Finally, he turned to God for help and asked what he had to do to save himself.

"Cut the rope," came the reply. He refused and they went on like this through the night. There was no way God, any God in Heaven, could tell him to cut the rope that was his only thread left to life.

"Trust me," replied the voice, "cut the rope."

He couldn't do it.

They found him frozen solid the next morning, dangling three feet off the ground.

Our fears are nothing more than doubts, and even with nothing left to lose, most of us cling to our doubts, rather than let go of our egos and grasp onto certainty.

MOVING HEAVEN AND EARTH

Meditate on a Specific Situation You Want Changed and What Outcome You'd Like to See

קרע שטנ

As my teacher reminded me, this line works particularly well to control negative external forces, including people who are obstinate or bureaucrats who refuse to process our papers. If you want to go to the front of the line, use this second line, meditating on the situation at hand. As Rav Berg says, it literally has "the power to move events." It takes the stress out of life.

THE JUSTICE SYSTEM

Speaking of bureaucratic systems, as Gina's mother-in-law was experiencing, few things spin slower than the wheels of justice, and since this line connects directly to judges, as explained above, it's the perfect line to use when facing the legal system. Gina's mother-in-law had been at odds with her well-off ex-husband for years. She'd also been in court with him for as many years, and the ordeal had not only drained her physically, but had wiped her out financially. He wouldn't pay a dime and her expenses kept racking up. There was nothing left. She had no money, no assets, and no place to live—no way to pay the rent, let alone eat. Her case dragged on and on, motion after motion, one setback after another.

Gina and her husband did what they could to help, but lawyers are expensive and they had their own family to care for. One day, Gina decided to do more. She sat down with her mother-in-law and they did the Genesis Prayer together, over and over again, meditating for deliverance from this endless legal cycle and her impoverished state.

Later that morning, Gina and her mother-in-law were in for a shock. They arrived at court as usual, but instead of the typical runaround, the judge announced, "Enough," and rendered a verdict. He awarded Gina's mother-in-law a huge sum of money and ordered her ex-husband to pay all her legal fees. *(Bli ayn hara.)* When Gina told my wife this story she acknowledged that nothing changes destiny the way the Genesis Prayer does. It's true. It's also true that justice only moves slowly on the physical plane. On the spiritual level, justice is instantaneous, which is why the Genesis Prayer can greatly speed things up for us; it helps us tap into an alternate reality, injecting mercy into our lives and true justice into our trials.

~~~~

As happened to my wife and me on the freeway in L.A., and with Graham on the plane, and as has happened to us and our acquaintances dozens of times in getting taxis at impossible hours and locations, reality shifted and we got where we needed to be when we needed it. I can recall distinctly two clear occasions on which my wife, Debbie, and I had fallen into that dreaded no man's land around 4:30 in the afternoon when all the taxis switch shifts en masse, and in their rush to get home they all go off-duty at once. We had our baby with us and were quite a walk away from home. It wasn't the end of the world, but nonetheless, it was a stiff inconvenience after a heavy day of shopping. As stated previously, it's not the intention of the Creator—Light, life force, or however you're most comfortable addressing it—for us to be inconvenienced; it's not the nature of the universe. We did a quick Genesis Prayer together, emphasizing this second line, and watched as a taxi flicked off its off-duty light and swerved across all four lanes of Madison Avenue to stop right in front of us. What made the scene so much more remarkable is that he swerved away from other potential passengers also frantically waving for cabs. They were dumbfounded.

On another occasion the driver didn't even know what he'd done. At first he wouldn't let us in the cab, as he repeated over and over that he'd intended to pick up the guys across the street, not us. They had no way of knowing his intentions; he'd sped right past them and pulled up right in front of us. They already had their backs to him and were flailing their arms, trying to hail another cab. He argued with us aggressively for two minutes, but in the end, the stubborn, disoriented driver had no choice but to submit to the will of the universe.

I'm not gloating, God forbid, and I could understand if you thought our good fortune of knowing the Genesis Prayer came at the expense of others, but that's where seeing the big picture comes in—or in this case, not seeing it. The spiritual tools of the universe never work to the detriment of others, and even though it appears that they may seem to fly in the face of our moral sensibilities and the spirit of fair play, the universe isn't a zero-sum game; there are no losers. As for those people who were left on the street corner, their lives didn't end there; that incident is one tiny step in their endless journey. Just because we can't see what blessings were concealed in their temporary misfortune doesn't mean they weren't in store for them. Maybe they continued shopping and found the deal of their lives, or maybe they tired of walking and stopped for coffee, where they met a soul mate. We have no way to know, but we do know that the Light Force will not harm someone.

It's not just us. Everyone we know who's tried the Genesis Prayer in thick traffic or to get a taxi in the rain has had tremendous success. Some people call it luck, others miracles. It's worked so well for our friends Carmela and Julio that when they call their car services all the drivers fight over them—they all want a part of that magic, as they call it, to breeze into the city.

In the first line, we opened a gateway, a pathway to certainty and to the limitless realm. In the second, we've shut down the gates that lead to doubt and set aside all our limitations. In the next line we're balancing out the powerful energy we're receiving and connecting to beauty, called *Tiferet,* the next dimension. The first line carries the energy of Abraham, the second of Isaac, and the third represents Jacob, a unifying force that by putting our consciousness in the frame of compassion helps us to come from the right place and thus make the right decisions whenever they come up. We begin by saying *"Tiferet,"* and asking Jacob, the Patriarch, for his help, understanding, and merit: *"Bizhoot Yaakov Avinu."*

11

Line 3—Sustenance, Healing, and Protection

TIFERET/GLORY AND BEAUTY/JACOB

ɔmrem Kevavat	Yichudechah Dorshay	Gibor Na	(*Tiferet*)	3 ←
כבבת שמ	דור שי יחודך	נא גבור	(תפארת)	3 ←
	יכש	נגד		
←	Shin Caf Yud	Dalet Gimmel Nun		←

Summary Meditations

The asterisks indicate the most important ones

נגד   *Give Us This Day Our Daily Bread
(Meditate to receive sustenance through sharing and/or tithing, or to form a partnership with the universe)

יכש   *Forgive Us Our Trespasses
(Ask that your sins and negative thoughts and deeds get purged at the seed level from your psychological, emotional, physical, and spiritual states)

יכש   *Purification and Healing
(Meditate on this sequence entering your body as a pinprick of bright white light chasing out any darkness

harbored inside, then envision the light spreading rapidly
from cell to cell, organ to organ, until your whole body is
glowing bright white and all the negativity has dissipated
into the atmosphere, leaving you in perfect health. Repeat on
others you care about, and on your community as a whole,
then on any trouble spots in the world, such as the Mideast.)

שׁדי   Protect Us This Day
(Meditate that this Name of God stays with you all day
and is at the entrance to all your dealings, and ask that it
protect you from any negative forces)

נגב שׁדי   A Secret Gateway to Knowledge and Glory
(Meditate that you connect with the Archangel Metatron
and ask for any knowledge that can help you in your spiritual quest)

As always, the first letter of each of the six words corresponds
to the six meditative letters of the line נגד יכשׁ. As instructed by
the sages, we're going to split the sequence into its two triplets for
meditative purposes. First we meditate on the first triplet:

Dalet Gimmel Nun   נ ג ד   ←

GIVE US THIS DAY OUR DAILY BREAD

Meditate to Receive Sustenance Through Sharing and/or Tithing, or to Form a Partnership with the Universe

When we total up the value of the letters in this combination it
works out to 57, which is equivalent in Hebrew/Aramaic to *zan,* sustenance. The sages tell us we can use this coded triplet to draw down
sustenance of all types—wealth, health, and relationships—into our
lives. There is a catch, though. According to the Pentateuch and the
sages, it's sustenance through sharing and tithing. Only by sharing
can we draw a continuous and endless stream of the Light (life)
Force of God into our beings and lives. We're like sinks with
plugs in the bottom: we can be filled with any temperature water we

like, but we can only hold just so much, and then we make a mess of things. When we remove the plug, our blockages, the water can flow through us endlessly. It's the same with the Light Force. If we remove our blockages—the second triplet on this line, the "*Yud Caf Shin*" (יכש), helps us to do just that—and share with others through our actions and charity, we can make ourselves open channels to receive endless blessings in our lives.

ای

BREAKING THE CODE

That this connection is made at this level, under the auspices of the energy of Jacob, is no coincidence. Even though Abraham and Isaac also tithed, Jacob was the first to make such a vow to the Lord and separate a tithe from his income. Because a tithing is 10 percent, it's no coincidence that Jacob had to spend 21 years with *Laban,* the biblical representative of all that was darkness and evil, and that the Israelites had to spend 210 years in the darkness of exile in Egypt; after all, the exile began when Jacob and the seventy members of his family entered it. Moreover, the ordinal value of בנד is 21.

ای

FORGIVE US OUR TRESPASSES

Ask That Your Sins and Negative Thoughts and Deeds Get Purged at the Seed Level from Your Psychological, Emotional, Physical, and Spiritual States

ای

BREAKING THE CODE

Encoded into the mathematics of this line are the values 22 and 220, and not only did the end of the 220 years of exile in Canaan coincide with Jacob entering Egypt, it also coincided with the end of the 22 years that Jacob spent in the darkness of his grieving for his supposedly dead son Yosef. This 22 versus 220 is also 10 percent and yet another allusion to tithing, but more important, we have a shifting in our consciousness of the journey that the Genesis Prayer is taking us on.

꙰

We're at a special juncture in our simultaneous journey through the Genesis Prayer and the Bible. We're through with the cleansing process and moving out of our accumulated darkness and into the light. Just like the three Patriarchs—who correspond to the first three lines of the Genesis Prayer—their families, and the Israelites, our journey takes us away from the darkness of idol worship and materialism toward the Creator and the Light. To the sages, idol worship was a code word, not for stone figurines, but for all the materialistic elements in our lives that hold us captive: money, drugs, sex, alcohol, carbs—anything for which we can't control our cravings, or anything that means so much to us that we're willing to step on others to get it. Our fears also represent idol worship because they hold us captive. We need to be able to restrict and say no to them, all of them, not as a moral issue, not entirely; no one is saying we should give up sex or having money, but we need to be able to stop their hold over us. The only way to regain our free will is to let go, to push these overpowering desires and needs away. The Genesis Prayer and the next sequence help us to do that.

Shin Caf Yud   י כ ש   ←

Yud Caf Shin (י כ ש) can help us to return all the cells in our body to their embryonic state, the undifferentiated state they were in when we were first conceived, before any chaos, stress, or negativity could enter and impact them. The *Zohar,* written nineteen hundred years ago, explains that negativity, whether internally or externally generated, corrupts the inner makeup of our cells—what we'd call DNA. By using the *Yud Caf Shin* (יכש) we don't become embryos again, but our cells shake off that accumulated negative energy, working out the kinks built up over the years, which in a sense give us a fresh start. Modern physicists concur that our DNA and many of our cells' proteins are tightly wound up springs, and like all springs the right vibrations can loosen them up and shake out the kinks.

This triplet (יכש) has the numerical value of 330, which is the same as the word *Shal*, transgression. We know from the sages that this is the most powerful sequence there is for removing the impact of our transgressions on our lives and health.

PURIFICATION AND HEALING

Concentrate on Healing at All Levels, Physical, Emotional, Psychological, and Spiritual, as You Do the Meditation Prescribed Below, Leaving You in Perfect Health. Repeat on Others You Care About, and on Your Community as a Whole, Then on Any Trouble Spots in the World such as the Mideast.

In our seminars, we usually lead people through a mini-purification meditation in which you are instructed to picture the *Yud Caf Shin* (יכש) entering a single cell of your body as a bright white light, chasing out any darkness that may be there, and visualize the bright white light of the *Yud Caf Shin* (יכש) spreading rapidly like a benevolent virus from cell to cell, organ to organ, until your entire body is glowing bright white. You should be able to feel the warmth that you're radiating into the universe. You should picture any darkness dissipating and disappearing into the atmosphere forever. You should then repeat the visualization, meditating on other people you care about.

Since the *Yud Caf Shin* (יכש) has the power to take you back in time, so to speak, you can use it as a spiritual cleansing *mikve* to remove any emotional and psychological scars you've incurred at any time since your birth; you can use it to remove any darkness or disease, physically or spiritually. Because this line has this power to remove negativity at the seed, or most fundamental, level, you can go back or, as we explained before, temporarily shift yourself to an earlier universe and remove the cause of disease long before it can manifest in your body.

We can use this line to cleanse our all those seeds, all the agglomerations of our reactivity, our negative actions, and even our negative thoughts. No one wants to be the person who unwittingly caused a war—imagine the bad karma—but we don't want to be the person who caused someone to get angry one day and thus caused them to get cancer twenty years later or, God forbid, get it ourselves. Everything snowballs; it's a law of the universe, physical and metaphysical. Remember the butterfly beating its wings: eventually that tiny breath of anger will create a tempest somewhere, so we want to have a way to remove the anger before it grows.

As we complete the third line, we find that the *Yud Caf Shin* (יכש) was the third spiritual cleansing *mikve* in the Genesis Prayer, after the *Ana* (אנא) of the first word of the first line, and after the אקב of the first letters of the first three lines. Not only do these three spiritual *mikves* afford us opportunities to cleanse ourselves of negativity, these spiritual *mikves* enhance the powers of all the individual meditations, such as the *Yud Caf Shin*'s (יכש) power to rejuvenate and replenish all the sparks of life that we've lost beneath these dark husks *(Klippot)*.

There's yet another reason for these cleansing baths, or spiritual baptisms, and that is that they are preparing us for the next levels, where the really powerful miracles come from. The higher we climb spiritually, the more miracles we'll see, but also the purer we need to be. The Genesis Prayer is designed to take us to the highest levels, just as it did the sages, and everything we need to reach those exalted planes is built right into it. We'll point out the connections as we go. Most of them you can store away in the back of your consciousness, where they'll be readily accessible to you every time you do the Genesis Prayer, activated only by your visual connect with the letters at the end of each line. The technology is so complex, yet the process is so simple for us.

Gill, the chairman of a large insurance company, takes advantage of this technology all the time, especially the healing properties of the *Yud Caf Shin* (יכש). He's been doing the Genesis Prayer for thirteen years, receiving innumerable miracles along the way, but he told me specifically of one that happened when he'd first learned the prayer—the miracle of sight. An assistant of his had such terrible migraines that they caused one of her eyes to tear up and shut tight. The doctors were helpless against her agony and plight, but under Gill's quick tutelage she recited the Genesis Prayer and opened both her eyes. The tears stopped at once, and Gill and his grateful assistant were immediately convinced of the prayer's power. While the gift of sight is amazing and migraines can be devastating, Gill credits the Genesis Prayer with helping to heal many more serious illnesses. *Bli ayn hara.*

BREAKING THE CODE

The sages describe a process whereby with the right meditation the *Yud Caf Shin* (יכש) can strengthen our immune systems to root out disease for us, a process akin to building fresh stem cells in our bodies, which is interesting because our scientists tell us that stem cells are found within our bone marrow, and as we know from the sages, the **42** letters of the Genesis Prayer connect with the **42** joints in our bodies, and the 248 total letters and words in the full Genesis Prayer connect with the 206 bones in our bodies together with the **42** joints that link them (206 + **42** = 248).

If you have the time and you want to get the most out of the connection, you can expand your channel of sharing and thus the energy flowing through you by meditating on others as Gill does, or expand it further by meditating on the major places of negativity around the world, such as the Mideast, sending them the white healing light of the *Yud Caf Shin* (יכש) and helping to relieve some of the pressure on the planet.

PROTECT US THIS DAY

Meditate That This Name of God Stays with You All Day and Is at the Entrance to All Your Dealings, Protecting You from Any Negative Forces

שׁדי

Let's take a look at the sequence נגד יכש and try to imagine what the sages saw so long ago. One of the most common forms of decryption the sages used was permutations, the rearranging of the letters in a word or phrase to reveal secrets concealed within. Since all words with the same root letters come from the same energy source, they knew there was always a possibility that a sequence of letters was doing double duty, and because most of the root letters were triplets (three-letter combinations), it would behoove them to search through the Genesis Prayer's triplets. I can imagine them laughing with joy when they found this one. It may be *the* most known triplet in Hebrew. On the doorpost of nearly every Jewish home is a *mezuzah* with the letters שׁדי *(Shin Dalet Yud)* on it. This triplet stands for the well-known Name of God for protection from evil, *Shaddai,* the Almighty. A visual connection with the שׁדי lasts all day, depending on the negative actions we commit or draw to ourselves with our consciousness. But if we stay in the right frame of mind, it won't abandon us. A doorpost can be metaphysical as well. We can place the שׁדי figuratively on any and all entrances we pass through, even things like the entrance to our computers via the Internet, and of course to our five senses. And with all the negativity in the world, we can use all the protection we can get.

According to the sages, the combination שׁדִּי is also a heavenly gateway, but to what?

A SECRET GATEWAY TO
KNOWLEDGE AND GLORY

Meditate That You Connect with the Archangel Metatron and Ask for Any Knowledge That Can Help You in Any Way

שׁדִּי כגנ

Imagine what the sages must have thought when they discovered that this possible portal to the beyond was hidden right there in the third line of the Genesis Prayer, the most important prayer in the Bible. One of the first tools they would have used would have been *gematria,* and the most basic form of *gematria* gives שׁדִּי a value of 314, which they would have known immediately is the value of the Archangel Metatron, the guardian of knowledge and the archangel responsible for the physical world, the one the Genesis Prayer is designed to help us control. According to the ancient texts at their disposal, Metatron was also Enoch, who gave us the Genesis Prayer. This would have been tantalizing for them, a gateway to limitless knowledge, but they'd want to have corroborative evidence before pursuing it further, so they'd have to examine the rest of the line. So when they subtracted (שׁדִּי) from (נגד יבשׁ) and were left with (כגנ), they saw right away that not only does (כגנ) spell "like the *Gan*", or *garden,* as in "like (as) *Gan Eden,* or Garden of Eden," but numerically the three remaining letters (כגנ) total 73, the same as the word *Chochma,* which is the highest dimension attainable and which means Wisdom. They'd know for sure that they'd discovered a gateway to knowledge and wisdom.

~

BREAKING THE CODE

The sum of the numerical values of all seven words in the Bible's first verse, the one that the Genesis Prayer is derived from, connects to 73 and *Chochma* in that it's 2701, which is the precise sum of all the integers from 1 to 73, in other words 73 + 72 + 71 + 70 . . . or Σ(1–73). This is surely no coincidence, as the sum of the Torah occurrences of the fourth, second, and fifth words of that same verse is also 2701. In other words, the number of times the words and (את, ברא, and השמים) are collectively repeated in the Torah total 2701, just like the sum of the values for all seven words of that verse. These three words translate to "Created with the Heavens." Moreover, further evidence of the intentional design is that the fourth and second words of the Bible have a total of 2,628 occurrences in the Torah, and 2628 = Σ(1–72), or the sum of all the integers through 72.

~

So we know that 73 is the value of *Chochma* ("wisdom")and what that means for us, but how can we be sure that 73 wasn't meant to be the value for something else? Because making strong spiritual connections requires having certainty and accessing a gateway involves knowing what it really connects to, how do we know that 73 wasn't meant to stand for something else? Well, the Torah is nothing if not redundant, and we never have to rely on the word of a single sage or the revelations of a single equation. We can see this redundancy at work in the box below, where the depth of meaning provided by simple math and the providence of the sages serves to booster our level of certainty.

~

BREAKING THE CODE

Well, the Torah is nothing if not redundant, and 2701 is not only the sum of the integers through 73, but 2701 = 73 × 37, and 37 is not only the value of the highest of the five levels of soul *(Yechida)*, but 37 is also the sum of the ordinal positions of the letters in *Chochma* (חכמה), which as we've said has the numerical value 73. In other words, the positions of the four letters of *Chochma* within the Hebrew/Aramaic alphabet—eighth, eleventh, thirteenth, and fifth respectively—add up to 37. (See Appendix Two for a chart.) Now, knowing this, the meaning to the sages and to us couldn't be clearer, as 73 + 37 = 110, for as we'll see in the coming verses of the Genesis Prayer, 110 is the value of the word *nes* ("miracle"), which is what this first verse of the Bible is meant to bring us. All we need is the interface of the Genesis Prayer to draw them out.

~

Moreover, because other sages have told us that this sequence connects us to the Throne of God, to which Metatron is guardian, we can see how powerful this line is to us and was to them. Because they tell us this sequence is the bridge between our world and the Tetragrammaton, or God, we can understand that the whole process will bring us closer to God and to the power of miracles, abundance, and the wisdom inherent in this line. This sequence is one of the deepest mysteries revealed to date. The second-century *Zohar* tells us it connects to the wisdom of King Solomon.

12

Line 4—Blessings

NETZACH/VICTORY/MOSES

Gomlem Tamid	Tsidkatechah Rackamay	Taharem Barckem	(*Netzach*)	4
תמיד גמלם	רחמי צדקתך	ברכם טהרם	(נצת)	4
צתג		בטר		
Gimmel Tav Tsaddie		Resh Tet Bet		←

Ask for the support, leadership, and merit of Moses (Bizhoot Moshe Rabbeinu)

Summary Meditations

The asterisks indicate the most important ones

רצ   Meeting Our Soul Mates at the Well of Miriam
(Meditate that you've traveled through a cosmic gateway and are at the Well of Miriam. You want to sip from the water and ask to meet your soul mate, not just your marriage one, but the others with whom you should do business, have friendships, and so on.)

רצ   Fulfilling Our Desires
(List your spiritual desires or concentrate on one of them and ask that they [or it] be fulfilled)

רצ   Strengthening Our Relationships and Being One Soul
             (Meditate to strengthen all your relationships, including
             with humanity, to help draw in your soul mates.)

רצ   The Power of Praying for Others—The Miracle of
             Conception
             (Meditate that you're at the Well of Miriam and that
             you want your spouse to have a healthy child or to con-
             ceive, as the case may be. Even more powerful is to medi-
             tate that everyone who wants to conceive gets to.)

בט רצ תג   *Getting the Perseverance to See Things Through to
             the End
             (Ask for the willpower and perseverance to see things
             through to victory, to achieve your goals, especially the
             ones you set at the outset of the Genesis Prayer)

בט רצ תג   *Receiving the Power to Succeed
             (Meditate to receive the will to succeed, to get the
             Olympian spirit, and to see past the obstacles)

A COSMIC GATEWAY

As the sages stared at the sequence that makes up this line
(בטרצ תג), and as they drew upon the knowledge absorbed
through the previous line, they would have realized that the two
letters in the middle of the line (רצ) had a value of 290, the same
as Moses's sister, Miriam. Then, as they meditated further, they
would have also noticed that the pair of letters (רצ) was smack in
the middle of the Prayer.

This may have been the clue that prompted them to look
further—we can only speculate. What they found, though, was that
this central position corresponded with the structure of the Torah (or
Pentateuch) scroll itself. For starters, they all knew that the numbers
of columns (248) in the Torah scroll plus the number of rows (**42**)
in it was also 290. Since **42** always represents the Genesis Prayer, the
42-letter name of God, it's my guess that that's what guided them to
the connection initially. Be that as it may, trial and error or divine

inspiration would have eventually led them to the equation $(248 \times 42)/358 = 29.0^+$, and since 358 is the numerical value for the word "Messiah" *(Mashiach),* and since to the sages 29.0 and 290 are essentially equivalent, and moreover since the small *gematria* value of רצ is 29, they would have realized how important this connection is.

In fact, they would have realized that they'd happened upon yet another significant gateway. There are only a couple dozen words/numerical values that held any great significance for the sages, so when they found a connection to one, it wasn't a coincidence. Because they had no computers or calculators, they mostly relied on intuition and divine guidance to come up with their calculations, and then parchment and ink only to reconfirm them.

BREAKING THE CODE

The graphic relationship between the Genesis Prayer and the Pentateuch (Torah) is anchored at the very heart of the **42**-letter matrix, through the רצ, where it can simultaneously draw upon all the letters, be they in pairs or triplets, where it can channel through to us the entire structural power of the Pentateuch, zeroed in like a crosshairs, 248 columns by **42** rows, leading us to the Messiah.

There was yet another clue given to sages that the Genesis Prayer's central pair צר is a secret gateway through which all the collective energy of all **42** rows and all 248 columns of the Pentateuch flows, and that is that the letters צר are used as a *word* only once in the entire Torah. It's found in Genesis 18:7, and the sages knew there are 187 total chapters in the Torah. Moreover, the names of the two letters צר, or *Resh* and *Tsaddie,* plus their *Kolel* is 616, the numerical value for the word "The Torah" itself, whose square root is 24.8, as in the 248 letters and words of the full Genesis Prayer. Therefore, we see, as the sages did, that this axial central pair (צר) is simultaneously representative of the total number of chapters, columns, and rows in the Torah and of "The Torah" itself.

Once open, this secret gateway is like a cosmic well through which all the energy of our universe wells up and rushes forth, surging out in a spiraling motion, 22 letters counterclockwise, 22 letters clockwise, the yin and yang at the exact spiritual center of the Genesis Prayer and of the universe itself. That this secret gateway is found at the heart of the Genesis Prayer is no coincidence. Abraham called this gateway the link to the "Heart of Heaven"; physicists call it a cosmic worm tunnel; mathematicians, a Fermat Spiral.

According to the first-century *Sefer HaBahir,* (the *Book of Illumination*), through this heart pass the 32 Paths of Wisdom that one ascends in order to enter the spiritual dimension, and according to the even more ancient *Book of Raziel,* this Heart is the "Heart of Heaven," the place where God spoke to Moses through the fire on Mt. Sinai. Because the numerical value of the word "heart" is 32 and the total numerical value of this line is 32 × 22, we see that the sages knew exactly where to find this gateway to the "Heart of Heaven": right at the crossroads of the 22 letters. Because the word for heart, *lev,* also means "middle," "core," "center," and "courage," this connection of the sages is even more convincing.

FROM ABRAHAM'S *SEFER YETZIRAH*

"Twenty-two Foundation letters: He engraved them, He carved them, He permuted them, He weighed them, He transformed them, And with them, He depicted all that was formed and all that would be formed." And later in the book: "These are the twenty-two letters with which He engraved *Ehyeh, Yah, YHVH, El ohim, YHVH Tzavaot, Elohim Tzavaot, El Shaddai, YHVH Adonai,* and with them He made three Books, and with them He created His universe . . ." There are multiple interpretations of the three Books, one of which is the three columns of the Genesis Prayer, whose total number of elements (lines, meditation letters, pairs, triplets, words, and letters in the words) is 333.

To the sages and to us this is the place to mend broken hearts, metaphysically and metaphorically; to get to the "heart" of a matter; and to seek out what's truly in our hearts. The well initiated

תצ	גי	אב
טנ	עש	כר
כש	די	נג
תג	רצ	בט
נע	בט	חק
זק	לפ	יג
ית	וצ	שק

can picture the spiral and pass through its central portal, and the rest of us can meditate on the צר, and ask for our hearts and convictions to be strengthened.

To the sages it was also a secret entrance—one that takes two keys to open. We've just received the first, the knowledge of where it is and what it leads to; the second key we have to earn with our consciousness. The more we do the Genesis Prayer and follow the meditations, the more we'll shift our consciousness. The more we share and show the universe we have true appreciation, the more the Genesis Prayer will do for us. It's a magnificent spiral we're riding toward spirituality and true fulfillment. But it's not enough just to say we have certainty, we have to feel it inside us, and that takes work. The Genesis Prayer will make that work easier.

We've been given so many gifts by the Creator, but we should never forget that we need to show our appreciation by sharing those gifts with others. When we share something with someone from our hearts and not from our calculating minds we're touching something inside them, awaking a spark of light that will create a chain reaction of goodwill in the universe, and as a cause of all this goodwill, we reap enormous spiritual benefits. Be proactive, tell people what you've found, show them, go that extra mile, do all the things you've learned that will bring you closer to the Light and them as well. There's no such thing as being selfish in terms of our desire for the Light Force of God. The more we want it, the more we earn it, the closer we'll get.

THE WELL OF MIRIAM

Meditate That You've Traveled Through a Cosmic Gateway and Are at the Well of Miriam. You Want to Sip from the Water and Ask to Meet Your Soul Mate, Not Just Your Marriage One, but the Others with Whom You Should Do Business, Have Friendships, and So On.

The more we share the more we get, which is why I'd like to share with you a powerful secret about that gateway, that secret entrance at the heart of the Genesis Prayer. The sages knew it had a name: the Well of Miriam. They knew that the pair רצ numerically translates to "Miriam," and that through its roots it decodes to the word *well*, and moreover that it literally spells out the word "running" (רצ) as in the angels, or messengers, running back and forth. This place of angels "running and returning" is alluded to in Ezekiel 1:14 and in Abraham's *Sefer Yetzirah*. Moreover, according to Abraham the צ, *Tsaddie* of רצ represents joy, happiness, miracles, wonders, and charity, and it has the same numerical value as *mayim*, water. We also know from Abraham and from the second-century *Zohar* that the ר, *resh* of רצ is equivalent to the full power of the Tetragram-maton, the ineffable Name of God (יהוה). Abraham also told us that the letter ר, *resh* connects to the planet Mercury, representative of the energy of speed and of being a messenger. It's through this well that all this abundance flows rapidly like water, flows right to us, and all we have to do is walk up and take a sip, just as the Is-raelites did as they wandered through those **42** places in the desert and sipped from the Well of Miriam, their constant companion.

SOUL MATES

רצ

List Your Spiritual Desires or Concentrate on One of Them, Like Meeting Your Soul Mate, and Ask That They (or It) Be Fulfilled

Moreover, the letters רצ are at the root of the Hebrew/Aramaic word *ratzon*, רצון, meaning "desire," indicating that this well is the source of fulfillment of our spiritual desires. But there's an even a big-ger secret waiting for us at Miriam's Well, and that's that it's at this well that all the Patriarchs met their soul mates. It's the place where we can, too. A friend of mine, Marco, not too long ago asked me to pray that he'd find his soul mate. He is a very quiet, spiritual guy, the strong silent type, but he hadn't had a date in the years I'd known him. Instead, I directed him to the רצ in the Genesis Prayer and instructed him to meditate that he was at the Well of Miriam, where he could ask for his soul mate himself. Within two weeks my wife told me that Marco was seeing someone. I know they've been together for the past few months *(Bli ayn hara),* and God willing it'll lead to marriage.

For most of us our highest spiritual desire is bonding with our soul mate and in this way we can elevate even higher together, but there are many other spiritual goals and desires. As the sages have shown us, the combination רצ connects to "desires" and also to "running," as in the angelic messengers running back and both, carrying our acknowledged desires with them and bringing us the means of fulfillment in return. All we need to do is make those desires—for a soul mate, for good-hearted friends, for good relationships, for good healthy children, for success and wealth for us to share with, for less hassles so we can have more time with which to help others, for safety, health, peace, and so on—known. In other words, let the universe know we've awakened.

STRENGTHENING OUR RELATIONSHIPS AND BEING ONE SOUL

רצ

Meditate to Strengthen All Your Relationships, Including with Humanity, to Help Draw in Your Soul Mates

When we do the Genesis Prayer and get to רצ on the fourth line, we should meditate that we're at the Well of Miriam and ask that we connect with our soul mate. If you're already married you can ask that your relationship with your spouse be blessed and strengthened. It's all about love. Remember, soul mate relationships aren't limited to spouses. They can be with business partners, mentors, best friends, and especially with our children. The רצ connection can strengthen all our relationships.

As stated at the outset of this book, the Genesis Prayer is derived from the first verse of the Bible, so it's no coincidence that the midpoint of the Genesis Prayer, the all-important *Resh-Tsaddie* (רצ)

combination is also the final two letters of that first verse, or the twenty-seventh and twenty-eighth letters of Genesis, and thus it's no coincidence that 27 + 28 = 55, which is the numerical equivalent of the word "bride" *(kallah)*. What better clue could the sages have had?

~

BREAKING THE CODE

Because 55 is one of the few numbers Abraham gave in his *Book of Formation (Sefer Yetzirah),* and moreover since the sages consider the Torah to be our "bride," it's one of the key trigger numbers for them. Now since the *resh* (ר) and the *tsaddie* (צ) of (צר) are the twenty-seventh and twenty-eighth, and also the last two, letters in the Bible's first verse, we can note as the sages did that the numerical word values 27 and 28 are found 83 and 82 times respectively in the Pentateuch (Torah), which is not only a powerful hint that both these letters are meant to be taken together, but because (27 + 83) = (28 + 82) = 110, the value for *Nes* (נס), or "miracle," the sages knew exactly what they could get from this gateway.

~

We all want to meet our soul mate; that goes without question. But why is this at the heart of the Genesis Prayer? It's because the purpose of the Genesis Prayer is to achieve unity and bring people together. In essence, the universe is an engine of giving; all we have to do is be willing to help ourselves.

As the saying goes, "You can lead a horse to water . . ." We have to be willing to drink.

We have to want to be one soul with everyone everywhere, and thus open to meeting our true soul mates, or we won't be able to recognize them when we do meet them. By meditating on being one soul and on being an integral part of the global and local community, our soul mate is sure to find us. By limiting our vision to a small circle of friends, we're most probably excluding our soul mates.

THE POWER OF PRAYING FOR OTHERS—
THE MIRACLE OF CONCEPTION

רצ

Meditate That You're at the Well of Miriam and That You Want Your Spouse to Have a Healthy Child or to Conceive, as the Case May Be. Even More Powerful is to Meditate That Everyone Who Wants to Conceive Gets to and That All the Souls Who Want to Come Down Get the Opportunity.

The sages tell us that the רצ pair represents and connects to Isaac (יצחק) and Rebecca (רבקה) and their spiritual bond. They further tell us that we should meditate for others as Isaac did for Rebecca and as Rebecca did for Isaac. When we meditate for others we make ourselves open channels for the Light Force to flow through us without limitations, and conversely, when we pray solely for ourselves, we're cutting ourselves off from the universe and can thus only absorb so much of all that it would like to give to us. Therefore they advise us to follow Isaac and Rebecca's example and to pray for our friends to meet their soul mates as well. And even better is to pray that everyone connects with his or her soul mate.

This spiritual philosophy holds true for everything in life, but what Isaac and Rebecca were praying for in particular was a child. You see, Rebecca didn't have a womb, yet their mutual prayers for each other helped Rebecca to conceive nonetheless. Just as the first three lines of the Genesis Prayer are designed to work together, so are the fourth and fifth lines. As Andrea found out, the Genesis Prayer is a powerful tool for conception. Today, with modern science coupled with the ancient tool of the Genesis Prayer, there's no reason any women shouldn't have the opportunity to conceive. The Bible made this very clear in that neither Sarah nor Rebecca had wombs, and nonetheless they conceived Abraham's son and grandson, our Patriarchs.

However you choose to attempt the meditations, you want to first meditate on bringing a soul into the world for unselfish reasons,

putting the welfare of the soul and child first and foremost. You
then want to meditate, as Isaac and Rebecca did, that they are doing
so for your spouse. Next you want to meditate that all your friends
who want to conceive do so—this removes any conscious or uncon-
scious jealousy from the process. If you're using a fertility clinic, you
want to meditate that everyone there conceives and brings their babies to full term as well. Finally, you want to meditate that everyone
who wants a child gets one, specifically a healthy one. The more inclusive and expansive your meditations, the more successful you'll be
because you're signaling to the universe that you're a higher soul
with a higher consciousness and thus ready to take on the responsi-
bility of taking care of and nurturing another soul.

SEEING THINGS THROUGH TO THE END

**Ask for the Willpower and Perseverance to See Things
Through to Victory, to Achieve Your Goals, Especially the Ones
You Set at the Outset of the Genesis Prayer**

The sages tell us this fourth line has been endowed with even
greater powers to help us. We want to meditate on the sequence

בטר צתג

and ask for help in seeing things through to the end. It makes sense
that this would be coupled with the meditation for finding our
soul mates because when we do meet them, we'll need it in order to
complete the relationship. Infused with the power of the entire
Pentateuch and the energy of Moses and Miriam, this line gives us
the boost we need not to give up. And as the sages tell us, the central pair (רצ) connects to the word *ratzon* (רצון), which not only
means desire, but "will" as in "willpower."

Far too often we give up in life, often only moments before we
were about to reach our goal. More often than not, it's not some
big insurmountable obstacle that's in our way, but some little

distraction or petty argument that our egos blow out of proportion. No matter what our goals are, it takes perseverance to achieve them. But when we're on spiritual paths, we're inadvertently asking for obstacles. Like anything in life, if it comes too easy, we don't appreciate it, so because spiritual goals are the highest ones, they are also the most difficult to achieve. All the tools we need to succeed in life are built right into the Genesis Prayer, and all we have to do is to be open to them. This perseverance is a hard nut to crack.

I can't tell you how many times in the past twelve years I've tried to get this knowledge out there—though I'm sure my wife can—and each time I ran into a brick wall, stopped cold by people who asked me, "Who cares about any of that?" or said, "It's only math," "Numbers are meaningless," "No one cares about spirituality," or any other number of excuses and rejections I got along the way. If at any time I'd given up and, instead of shoving aside my notes, I'd tossed them in the trash, you wouldn't be reading this today and millions of people wouldn't have had access to the awesome power and empowerment of the Genesis Prayer. Who knows what I'd be doing?

My teacher fared even worse. When he first started bringing out this knowledge, he and his family were attacked and beaten. Throughout history, the sages fought adversity, pain, and gruesome death to teach and pass on these powerful tools. In their quest to bring these connections to us the Ten Martyrs were alternately flogged, skinned, and/or roasted alive and crucified by the Romans at the time of the destruction of the Second Temple. At the heart of the stories of the patriarchs is their overcoming of tests and adversity. Nothing worth getting is gotten easily. That's why it's not easy to succeed, and why so few actually do.

That's why we need help to see things through to the end, whether it's finding our soul mates, getting wonderful children, or making a change in the world or in our lives. This fourth line will do that for us, give us the perseverance to battle our negative inclinations, laugh at the tests, and change our nature, and thus the nature of the universe around us. We all have the power within us, and this fourth line of the Genesis Prayer helps us to bring it out.

RECEIVING THE POWER TO SUCCEED

Meditate to Receive the Will to Succeed, to Get the Olympian Spirit, and See Past the Obstacles

The word *netzach* means "eternity," and the sages also define it as "victory," and more than just seeing things through to the end, this line helps us see them through to their successful conclusion; it imbibes us with the Olympian spirit, that spirit of striving for and getting the gold. This is the spirit for running faster at the end of the race than at the beginning, of never slowing down, of never thinking for a second that you can't win, of not knowing the meaning of defeat. This is the spirit of success, the one quality in common with all winners, all successful people. The rest of us pause and ponder while they go racing by. This line puts us on the fast track; it sets us up and propels us forward. All we have to do is set our sights high enough.

As we've seen encoded herein, this line also gives us the power to see things all the way through to the arrival of the Messiah.

The next line, *Hod,* corresponding to Aaron and having the aspect of Splendor, as the sages explain, holds the power to help us see beyond our five senses. We begin the meditations by asking that the merit of Aaron help guide us and enable us to see beyond our five senses (*Bizhoot Aaron HaCohen*).

13

Line 5—Seeing the Signs

HOD/SPLENDOR/AARON

datechah Nahel	Tuvchah Berov	Kadosh Khasin	(*Hod*)	5 ←
נהל עדת	ברוב טובך	חסין קדוש	(הוד)	5 ←
	טנע	חקב		
	Ayin Nun Tet	Bet Koof Chet		←

Meditative Sequences

The asterisks indicate the most important ones

חק   Developing Our Intuition
(Meditate to connect to and elevate our consciousness to
that of Sarah, Rebecca, Leah, and Rachel and to Enoch
in order to see things at a higher level, intuitively and
prophetically)

חקב   Connecting to Miracles and Prophetic Dreams
(Ask that you receive prophetic dreams through the merits of Jacob and Yosef. This is another opportunity to ask
for miracles.)

חקב טנע   *Receive Divine Inspiration and Developing a Sixth Sense
(Meditate to be able to draw upon the divine inspiration stored up in this cosmic level)

חקב טנע   *Understanding the Signs All Around Us
(Ask to be able to see and comprehend the signs that are all around you and to receive the inspiration to make the "right" choices in life)

חק   *Lead Us Not into Temptation/Seeing Past the Illusions
(Ask that Sarah, Rebecca, Leah, and Rachel help you to see past the illusions and temptations that cause you to make the wrong decisions in life)

INTUITION AND PROPHECY

חק

Meditate to Connect to and Elevate Our Consciousness to That of Sarah, Rebecca, Leah, and Rachel and to Enoch in Order to See Things at a Higher Level, Intuitively and Prophetically

Everyone knows women are more intuitive than men and we won't begin to go into why that is, but the two letters (חק) of the first column connect us at a glance to all four Matriarchs at once, and as we meditate on the חק of חקב טנע, not only can we ask them for help in all we do, but ask that they help raise our consciousness to their lofty level. Don't expect this simple meditation to make you a Matriarch, but it could set you on your way. The higher our consciousness ascends, the more we see. It's like climbing a tower and looking out: The higher you get, the bigger your scope of vision. Eventually, you'll be able to see what's coming over the horizon—this is called prophecy.

BREAKING THE CODE

The value of the two letters חק of the first column is 108, and the pure names of the Matriarchs are mentioned 108 times in the Pentateuch—Sarah, 28; Rebecca, 22; Rachel, 30; and Leah, 28. We can see, as the sages did, the secret code unfolding before us, one that unleashes the incredible intuitive powers of the four matriarchs. The technology of the Genesis Prayer and the Pentateuch (Torah) are so intertwined that there are no coincidences; they were designed to interconnect and build on one another.

One of the chariots of prophecy is Enoch, the same Enoch who brought us the Genesis Prayer. He was the first to prophesize of the giving of the Torah, the fall of the Temples, the coming of the Messiah, the Apocalypse, and much more. His first book, the one to contain all these prophecies, has 108 verses, connecting to the value of חק, 108, and obviously this is no coincidence, as who more than he would be aware of the values and codes within the Genesis Prayer? A further tie is found in the ח of חק because it's the first letter of the name Enoch. We can make the same connection we made with the Matriarchs with Enoch, elevating ourselves even higher.

HISTORIC CONTEXT

In case there are any doubts about the validity of the *Book of Enoch,* we should note that when the unadulterated Ethiopic Bible was discovered in 1773, it contained *1 Enoch* with its 108 verses, and moreover, that when the Dead Sea scrolls were found at Qumran, dating to 300 B.C.E, they contained seven large fragments of the *Book of Enoch,* all of which were identical to the Ethiopic Bible. We also know that the church fathers Tatian (110–172), Irenaeus, Bishop of Lyons (115–185), Clement of Alexandria (150–220), Tertullian (160–230), Origen (186–255), Lactantius (260–330), Methodius of Philippi, Miinucius Felix, Commodianus, Ambrose of Milan, and St. Augustine all approved and supported the Enochian writings, and that Tertullian even cited it as *"Holy Scripture."*

CONNECTING TO MIRACLES AND PROPHETIC DREAMS

Ask That You Receive Prophetic Dreams Through the Merits of Jacob and Yosef and That You Can Recall Them. This is Another Opportunity to Ask for Miracles.

There's lots more encoded in this line, not the least of which is the connection to Jacob's famous dream of seeing the angels go up and down the ladder in Genesis 28:12, for as the sages tell us, this connection helps connect us to the power of prophecy through our dreams. This connection to prophetic dreams is strengthened through the coded first triplet יעקב, whose sum is 110, as in the 110 years of Yosef, who came to control most of the wealth of the world, partially through his dream-interpreting skills. An added coded bonus is that 110 is also the numerical value for the word *nes,* miracle, which is what this line helps us to *see* when we get them. Too often we get miracles and don't recognize them for what they are. We can be so wrapped up in our own agendas that we ignore the superior plans the universe has in store for us. The universe helps let us know what's in store for us through our dreams, and this sequence not only helps us to remember our dreams, but also to elevate them to a higher level, especially if we do the prayer at night, and especially if we ask to receive messages/answers before going to sleep.

DIVINE INSPIRATION

**Meditate to Be Able to Draw Upon the Divine Inspiration
Stored Up in This Cosmic Level**

חקב מנע

Dreams and signs would require a separate discussion, but what's important for us to note as we meditate on the sequence חקב מנע is that we can use it to enhance our latent psychic abilities, to see not with our limited five senses, but with our sixth, helping us reach near-clairvoyant states of consciousness both while awake and while we sleep. It's revealed in the second-century *Zohar* that the dimension or spiritual level associated with the prior line, *Netzach,* together with this one, *Hod,* are the cosmic depositories of Divine Inspiration *(Ruach Hakodesh)* and are the places from which prophecy issues. We have an opportunity to tap into that divine inspiration by meditating on the sequence above. As you can see in the next two stories, this sequence can also increase your telepathic powers by acting as your antennae.

At a dinner recently I sat next to Mark McGuinness, and though he was mentally and spiritually vibrant, he's getting on in years and he misses his children terribly. As often happens with distance and growing families, their relationship has grown apart and Mr. McGuinness's thirty-six-year-old son *never ever* calls out of the blue, yet when Mr. McGuinness read over the Genesis Prayer and decided to write down the letters in order to commit them to memory, he'd only gotten as far as the first two letters of the first line when the phone rang. It was his son, calling to chat and renew their relationship. Already blessed with grandchildren, Mr. McGuinness considers this the greatest gift he could have received, and he fully credits the Genesis Prayer with this special miracle.

Yet another story of the mental telepathic powers of this prayer that comes to mind concerns Tara. When I'd finished the first draft of this book I asked her to review it for me and she did—on the subway to her office. Always a skeptic, Tara became eager to test out the Genesis Prayer for herself. It wasn't proof enough that she'd somehow managed to get a subway seat on a packed car, so she read the prayer and meditated on a friend she'd fallen out of touch with, hoping for the best. As she ascended the subway steps and her cell phone came into service, it rang. It was her friend. Tara's next call was to me.

Now, it's not going to happen for everyone this way, but since Mr. McGuinness's interests were pure and earnest in wanting to learn the prayer the best he could and because Tara was doing an altruistic act in helping me with the book, they got their prayers answered immediately.

UNDERSTANDING THE SIGNS
ALL AROUND US

Ask to Be Able to See and Comprehend the Signs
That Are All Around You and to Receive the Inspiration
to Make the "Right" Choices in Life

Our lives and world are filled with signs and choices, but most of us can't see the signs and thus don't make the right choices. The many crossroads in our lives come with at least one sign. Imagine driving in New York City and not knowing how to read or speak English; imagine how many parking tickets you'd get! That's what life is really like for us. Every stranger we bump into, every odd phrase we happen to overhear, every bit of unsolicited advice we receive is a sign and a message for us. Think of it as a map the universe provides us with to help steer us to a more spiritual path, to the path that will lead us to true fulfillment. Because we can't read it, we end up cursing the guy who bumped into us and/or saying, "Thanks, but no thanks," to the patronizing co-worker.

This world is a tough place, tougher yet if we try to be spiritual without a guidebook or road map. We need every bit of help we can get. We need the messages, we need the signs, and we also need a way to sift through them, and to know when and how to act on them. This is what the fifth line of the Genesis Prayer does for us. It gives us clarity in our life. It helps us filter through the confusion. And it puts the Matriarchs, the most knowledgeable, intuitive, piped-in, and sharing women in history, by our sides as we go through our days.

~

ANOTHER TURNING POINT IN OUR JOURNEY

The technology encoded into the Pentateuch (Torah) and the Genesis Prayer is limitless, and with each type of *gematria* the sages utilized, more revelations appeared. The various types of *gematria,* all variations of the same scale as presented in Appendix Two, allow each letter to be encoded with multiple meanings and purposes. As we said earlier, the sages had the advantage of divine inspiration to know which ones were the right ones, and rarely did a teacher add anything that hadn't been passed down to him from his teacher, thus ensuring the integrity of the connections they were taught to make. And of course, by now there have been thousands of years of trial and error to prove them correct. That's why when they tell us they used *gematria atbash*— an often-cited type of encrypted *gematria* cipher used by the sages in which the values of the alphabet are reversed with *alef* (א) = 400 and *Tav* (ת) = 1—in this fifth line to get a total of 430 as the sum of the two triplets (שמע + חקב), I don't question it. Neither do I doubt it when they say that this 430 represents the 430 years of total exile—220 in Canaan and 210 years in Egypt—that the Israelites experienced before receiving the Pentateuch.

Sure, 430 could mean other things that don't intuitively fit in with the flow of the journey the Genesis Prayer is taking us on, or with what it's trying to do for us. But with this line in the prayer, we've left Canaan and Egypt and completed the 430 years of total exile, and we've also left behind the Pharaoh Rameses, whose name carries the value 430 and whose darkness is legendary. Moreover, and more important, we've also left behind, or cleansed, the more animalistic part of our soul, the *Nefesh,* whose value is also **430**, and is the seat of all our selfish desires.

LEAD US NOT INTO TEMPTATION/ SEEING PAST THE ILLUSIONS

**Ask That Sarah, Rebecca, Leah, and Rachel Help You
to See Past the Illusions and Temptations that Cause You
to Make the Wrong Decisions in Life**

The technology in the Genesis Prayer is so beautiful and complex that even the lines are hermetically linked together to help us on our journey. The last letter of the fifth line and the first of the sixth spell out the word *chag* (חג), or "festival." At this point in the Israelites' journey they were asked to wait for Moses for 40 days, 40 always being the number assigned to prophecy and spiritual readiness in the Bible, but they didn't wait, and 6 hours shy of 40 days they constructed the golden calf, celebrating with a festival.

BREAKING THE CODE

Moses was summoned by God at the age of 40; 40 years passed before he stood in front of Pharaoh again; he spent 40 days and 40 nights with the Creator on Mt. Sinai, and he lived another 40 years; he recited *Deuteronomy,* the last Book, over 40 days; it rained for 40 days and 40 nights; the Israelites wandered in the desert for 40 years; Isaac was 40 when he married Rebecca; Esau was 40 when he married Judith; the spies searched the land for 40 days; Joshua was 40 when he took over from Moses; Solomon reigned for 40 years; David reigned for 40 years; and Eli reigned for 40 years. Also, according to the New Testament, Christ spent 40 days in the desert and rested for 40 hours in his tomb. Moreover, Mohammed received his first revelation at the age of 40; and Buddha began his mission at the age of 40.

In the Bible, this incident of idolatry was the ultimate temptation after the sin of Adam. Their evil inclinations couldn't hold out for another six hours and they had to create a golden calf to replace their faith in God, of whom they'd already witnessed so many magnificent miracles. The numerical value of the golden calf is 108, just like the first two letters of this fifth line. And as we've just seen, it's also the sum of the 108 recurrences of all the Matriarchs in the Pentateuch, meaning we've just been given yet another powerful gift: the power to help us overcome our temptations. As we've just explained, this line gives us the ability to see, and now we can understand that it's the ability to see when we're being tempted, led astray. It gives us the ability to see right from wrong, especially when we would otherwise be blinded by our own selfish desires.

That sets us up for the sixth dimension, *Yesod,* the foundation, the funneling down to our world of all the other dimensions, the one connected to the energy of Yosef the Righteous, at one point the most powerful man in the world. Like his father, Jacob, Yosef's energy is considered central column, and as such he imparts his quiet, peaceful energy to us through the Genesis Prayer's sixth line, and in particular through the pair of letters arranged in the central column (בל) of that line. The hidden code is that they total 110, as in the 110 years of Yosef's life. We begin the sixth line by saying *Yesod* and asking for the support and merit of Yosef, the Righteous *(Bizhoot Yosef HaTzaddik).*

14

Line 6—Drawing Down the Miracles

*Y*ESOD/FOUNDATION/YOSEF

K'dushatechah Zockray	P'nay L'amcha	Geh'eh Yackid	(*Yesod*)	

זוכרי קדושתך   לעמך פנה   יחיד גאה   (יסוד)

פ ז ק   יגל

Koof Zayin Pay   Lamed Gimmel Yud   ←

Summary Meditative Sequences

The asterisks indicate the most important ones

יג לפ זק   *Funneling Down the Energy of Miracles
(Ask Yosef to be your conduit for drawing down the miracles you've previously requested and any others that you may need but are unaware of)

יגל פזק   *Expanding Our Consciousness and Elevating Our Soul
(Make yourself a channel for spreading the wisdom of the Genesis Prayer to the whole world by meditating on everyone receiving it and on what actions you can take to share it with others)

יגל פוק   *Peace/Human Dignity/Messiah Consciousness
(Meditate on peace/human dignity/Messiah consciousness for all)

FUNNELING DOWN THE ENERGY OF MIRACLES

**Ask Yosef to Be Your Conduit for Drawing Down
the Miracles You've Previously Requested and Any Others
that You May Need but Are Unaware Of**

יגל פוק

The whole idea at the outset of this book was to draw miracles into our lives. All the prior meditations and connections have set us up for it. Now, at this level, is where that energy is downloaded in full force because of this level's double association with Yosef. Whoever Yosef worked for—the Midianite shopkeeper, Potiphar, Pharaoh, or his family—received enormous benefits, wealth, and miracles in their lives. We want to meditate on the sequence below and meditate on Yosef being our channel to draw down the energy of miracles.

The Genesis Prayer is divided into three columns, and Yosef is associated with the central column, and like the central filament in a lightbulb, this is the column through which all the energy is activated. And right in the central column of this line already associated with Yosef's central column energy is the pair לפ, which not coincidentally has the numerical value of 110, the same as Yosef's 110 years and as the word *nes* (נס) ("miracle"). So when we get to the pair לפ, we should meditate on drawing down all the miracles into our lives. This is the opening in the funnel that all the miracles meditated on above will pour down through, just as all the wealth and sustenance in the known world funneled down through Yosef in Egypt.

⌇

BREAKING THE CODE

According to the sages, there's 3 combinations of letters encoded into this line that numerically add up to the value of the word *nes* ("miracle"). The 3 combinations total 30 or 333, including the *kolel*, ק״ל, פ, and גוק. This is no coincidence, as we're told that in this 3-column balanced state the Divine Presence can energize and inspire us, which is why the sages say that this line and sequence of the Genesis Prayer brings inner peace, harmony, and balance into our lives.

⌇

EXPANDING OUR CONSCIOUSNESS AND ELEVATING OUR SOUL

Make Yourself a Channel for Spreading the Wisdom of the Genesis Prayer to the Whole World by Meditating on Everyone Receiving It and on What Actions You Can Take to Share It with Others

Yosef may be our channel, but in order to keep the floodgates open, the sages tell us we need to make ourselves part of that freely flowing energy of abundance and miracles by consciously sharing it with others. For this reason they tell us to meditate on making ourselves channels for spreading the wisdom of the Genesis Prayer and of the Messiah consciousness as we concentrate on the sequence *Yud, Gimmel, Lamed, Pay, Zayin, Koof*:

יגל פזק

In so doing we're expanding our consciousness, our ability to download the miracles. Numerically and visually this sequence connects us to the 231 Gates of Heaven as specified by Abraham in his *Sefer Yetzirah;* to the fully spelled-out Tetragrammaton; and to the full 187 chapters in the Torah.

～

The sages explain that the 2 triplets plus 2, the *kolel* (or "total") for the 2 triplets of this line, sum numerically to the four aspects/ levels of the Tetragrammaton (הה' וו הה יוד + הא' וא + יוד הי ויו הי + הי' ויו הי יוד + הא יוד + הי' ואו הי יוד) and thus help link us to an exalted level of consciousness. Also, the second triplet (פוד) has the numeric value **187**, connecting this line to the collective power of the full 187 chapters in the Torah.

～

That's a lot of power focused on a single line, and in order to process as much of it as possible and also to direct as much of it as possible toward the areas of our lives where we need it most, we want to make ourselves the biggest channels we possibly can. The best way to do that is to meditate that all these secrets of the Bible and of the Genesis Prayer reach everyone in the world, and moreover, that it all gets channeled toward the ultimate enlightenment, the ushering in of the Messiah *(Mashiach)* consciousness for the whole world. In so doing you're opening up all the floodgates and removing all the limitations that can block your fulfillment and your reception of multiple miracles.

As the sages have explained, we only get as much as we give, so we should also meditate that everyone on the planet gets the opportunity to share in the miracle-making power of the Genesis Prayer, and that we'll take the proactive step to spread the word to as many people as we can. Sharing is like a pyramid. Every time someone we shared the Genesis Prayer with gets a miracle we get one, too, and that includes all the people down the chain whom they shared it with as well. Every time we do the Genesis Prayer, that chain reaction of flowing positive Light gets reenergized, multiplying all of our connections many different ways.

There's so much energy flowing through this line, and only by sharing it can we receive its full benefits. Having free will, we are the masters of our fate and can choose exactly how many miracles we want to see and how big we want them to be. We can choose whether we want to let those dark husks of reactivity get in our way or not, whether we let doubts in through the small gates or not, and whether we keep the Genesis Prayer to ourselves or share it with as many people as we possibly can.

PEACE/HUMAN DIGNITY/MESSIAH CONSCIOUSNESS

Meditate on Peace/Human Dignity/Messiah Consciousness for All

יגל   פזק

Still meditating on the *Yud, Gimmel, Lamed, Pay, Zayin, Koof* (יגל פזק), we want to ask for peace for the world and for human dignity to extend to all humanity, for all people everywhere to receive the wisdom of the sages and the gifts given to all mankind that are hidden within the Bible.

A FINAL ENERGY BOOST

The architecture of the Genesis Prayer itself helps give our altruistic meditations a special energy boost. It's as if the Genesis Prayer was designed as a hologram. In a hologram, any part you look at contains the whole image imprinted on it. So when we do the prayer and are meditating on the pairs in the central column, or on the Expansion Sequence of the sixth line, or on the final triplet of the seventh line, we're actually receiving the full benefit of the entire prayer at once. This may be why people receive miracles who only remember one line, or who only get partway through the prayer. It may also be why the prayer gets more and more powerful the more connections/meditations on the various sequences we do. It's as if the prayer was designed to recharge and boost our connections at specific intervals, and probably at the precise moment when we'd need them most. We only understand a fraction of the intricate designs built into this magnificent prayer, but whatever we do grasp inspires awe. All we really need to know is that it works and that we're getting yet another powerful boost of energy as we leave the level of *Yesod* and drop down into the final level, our level, *Malckut,* the level of manifestation.

BREAKING THE CODE

We've discussed earlier how the sum of the central column of the Genesis Prayer is 903 and that 903 is the sum of all the integers from 1 to **42** and that the sages tell us that this means that all the powers of all **42** letters are channeled through this column to us. We find this same accumulation of all the power of all **42** letters again represented in this sequence, as the small *gematria*$_{(0)}$ value— the *gematria* scale used in numerical strings where *yud* (י) and *koof* (ק) are reduced to the value "0"—of the sum of the two triplets we're meditating on (יגל פֿ פֿוק) is 033 + 870, or 903. We'll see one more such agglomeration of the **42** letters as we finish reciting the last triplet of the seventh and last line, where the small *gematria*$_{(0)}$ value of that very last triplet (ציֿת) is also 903, subtracting the *kolel* (1). But remember, the three miracle sequences of this sixth line that add up to 333 are equivalent to the sum of all the letters, words, and meditative elements in the prayer.

15

Line 7—Manifesting All the Meditations

MALCKUT/KINGDOM/MANIFESTATION/ KING DAVID AND THE MESSIAH

Ta'alumot Yode'ah	Tsa'akatenu Ushma	Kahbel Shavatenu	(*Malckut*)	7
יודע תעלומות	ושמע צעקתנו	שועתנו קבל	(מלכות)	7

צית	שקו
Tav Yud Tsaddie	Vav Koof Shin

←

Meditative Sequences

The asterisks indicate the most important ones

יתצ - צית   We're in the House of God
(Meditate that the Genesis Prayer is the House of God, a House of Light, and that you're in it)

וצית   Wrapping Us in Light
(See the Genesis Prayer superimposed on an open Torah scroll made of white light and then see yourself wrapped up in it like a warm blanket of white light, a cocoon of bright white Light)

שקן ציח
Forever and Ever/The Eternal Light
(Meditate to draw in the Eternal Light by visualizing that you're in the Holy Temple in Jerusalem, aglow in the Light that comes from the time of creation and extends through you out toward eternity)

שקוצית
*Drawing the Light into Our World
(Picture your world as a well, and that all the energy of all the connections made above is pouring into it. Your body can also be a well or vessel for that energy.)

שקוצית
*Renewal/Starting Again
(Meditate on renewing all your relationships, including with the Creator, to start again fresh)

שקן צית
Receiving the Light
(Meditate to absorb the Light/energy into your body and mind)

ש ק ו צ י ת
*Thy Kingdom Come; Thy Will Be Done on Earth/Bringing the Messiah into Our Lives
(Visually connect with all **42** letters as a whole, and while looking at this seventh line, meditate to bring the limitless pure consciousness of the Messiah into your life and our world, the entire world)

שק
A Life Preserver in Desperate Times
(It's best if you visualize yourself donning burlap sackcloth and grieving for whatever it is you're lacking, but you can just meditate on the two letters as well)

שקן צית
*Manifesting All the Energy
(Meditate to manifest all the meditations you've done so that they all come through for you, and make a resolution to follow through)
We begin this last line saying Malckut, and asking that the merit of King David helps us to manifest all the connections (Bizhoot David Hameleck).

WE'RE IN THE HOUSE OF GOD

**Meditate that the Genesis Prayer is the House of God,
a House of Light, and That You're in It**

In at least five different ways this seventh line is represented by the number 46, meaning several different things, including "my God" and "God of," but it also represents the number of chromosomes in our DNA, thus connecting the Genesis Prayer through the *Malckut* or physical level to our physical essence, our DNA.

To ensure the protective properties of the Genesis Prayer and all the pure light and energy that it brings to us, the last line is embedded with special circular qualities that wrap the Genesis Prayer around us like a warm blanket of fresh light. The final three letters of the seventh line and thus of the whole prayer, צית, are the same as the final letters of the first line, ירצ, and they not only show the circular nature of the prayer, but also carry the value of 500, meaning "Be fruitful and multiply," which is what God said to Abraham, who corresponds to the first verse, and is also the wish God is giving to us, to be fruitful, as we finish the Genesis Prayer. If we add these two triplets together we get 1,000, representing *Keter,* the crowning dimension of God, and if we add the two other triplets that correspond to these two lines, we get 412, which is the value for *Beit,* or "house of," so these two lines together literally spell out "the House of God."

WRAPPING US IN LIGHT

**See the Genesis Prayer Superimposed on an Open Torah
Scroll Made of White Light and Then See Yourself
Wrapped Up in it Like a Warm Blanket of White Light,
a Cocoon of Bright White Light**

Moreover, the final four letters (וצית) of the seventh line just happen to be the same numerical value, 506, as the entire first line (אבגיתצ), and since the last three letters are the exact same ones as those of the first line, they are interchangeable and thus they inextricably tie the beginning to the end and the end to the beginning, making a perfect circle of protection for us.

Moreover, since there is no end and no beginning to the Genesis Prayer, the **42**-letter meditation becomes an energy field that encircles us invisibly, surrounding us like a supplemental aura that protects us and helps us attract positive forces into our lives while repelling the negative ones. Furthermore, the number 506 is the value of the word *Olat,* meaning elevating, which, as we said at the outset, is what the sages used the Genesis Prayer to help them do.

⤜

BREAKING THE CODE

Another example of the closed circuitry of the Genesis Prayer is found in its first and last words: *ana* and *ta'alumot,* **אנא** and **תעלומת**, which begin and end as the Hebrew/Aramaic alphabet does with *alef* (**א**) and *tav* (**ת**); moreover, the letters were both duplicated so we wouldn't miss the point of joining the beginning with the end, just as occurs in the Pentateuch's most common word value, 401, also comprised of *alef* (**א**) and *tav* (**ת**), and thus encapsulating all the power of all 22 letters wrapped into one. This concept is even reinforced by the reoccurrence of the word *et* (**את**), the most numerous in the Torah, which is found 2,622 times, since 26 is the value for the Tetragrammaton and 22 is the number of Hebrew/Aramaic letters in the *Alef-bet,* or "alphabet." It's also the fourth or middle word in the Bible's first verse, from which the Genesis Prayer is derived.

⤛

CONNECTING TO CREATION

So what came first, the Genesis Prayer with its fourteen triplets, or the Pentateuch itself? It's a chicken or the egg question. Was the Pentateuch built to encompass exactly 506 specific triplets, or were the triplets selected to fulfill a requirement of **506** occurrences in the Pentateuch? When we get to Part VI and see how integrated the Genesis Prayer is with the Pentateuch's first verse, we'll understand that the triplets and **42** letters couldn't have been selected after the Bible was written, but for now let's examine just the last two of those fourteen triplets.

FOREVER AND EVER/THE ETERNAL LIGHT

שקו   צית

Meditate to Draw in the Eternal Light, by Visualizing That You're in the Holy Temple in Jerusalem, Aglow in the Light that Comes from the Time of Creation and Extends Through You out Toward Eternity

When we multiply together the values of the two triplets of this seventh and last line, שקו × צית, we get **203000**, tethering us to Creation and to the Bible's first verse through the word ברא, *boreh* (203), "to create" or "to form," which is both the first three letters in Genesis, and also the entire second word of Genesis. Now, using the small *gematria atbash* cipher on the same two triplets, they translate numerically into **541 248**, whose alphabetical equivalents are Abraham (248) and Israel (541). And since Israel (541) is thus numerically the last word of the Genesis Prayer, and also literally of the Pentateuch (Torah), we have the first and last words of the Torah wrapped and tied together in the same line of the Genesis Prayer, the last line.

~❧

BREAKING THE CODE

The sages advise us that there is even more significance for us contained within the numerical value of that last triplet, **541**. Since the word value for "the heavens," 395, is found 146 times in the Pentateuch (Torah), and since 146 is the value for the word *olam*, meaning eternity, and since 395 + 146 = 541, the same as our final triplet, we're finishing up the Genesis Prayer with a connection to the heavens for eternity, and as we've just explained, also to Israel, Abraham (248), and Creation (203). Therefore, the final line of the Genesis Prayer is elevating us to a state where the beginning exists simultaneously with the end, and thus where everything is possible. And to reinforce that argument, the sages further point out that since 541 is the numerical equivalent of the sum of the first letters of the names of all 10 *sefirot* (dimensions), this last triplet is the realization of all the Light of all ten levels, implying that the **42**-letter prayer is a fully empowered and complete spiritual entity where everything exists at once and can be infinitely plucked—limited only by our consciousness.

꜀

It must also be noted that **248** is the numerical value for the archangel Raziel, whose book the *Sefer Raziel* gave us the Genesis Prayer in the first place and clued us in to all these wonderful gifts of the universe that were available.

We are at the end of our journey through the Genesis Prayer, which began with Abraham and the exile in Canaan; continued with Isaac, Jacob, and Yosef and the exile in Egypt; then on through the **42** places in the desert, guided by Moses and Aaron and nourished by the Well of Miriam; all along supported by the Matriarchs, Sarah, Rebecca, Leah, and Rachel; and we finally end up with God, represented by the fully expanded Tetragrammaton (248), in Israel (541) with our connection to eternity. Remember, this all took place within the first **42** letters of the Bible. Like an apple seed that holds the entire grown tree within its DNA, the first verse, through its counterpart, the Genesis Prayer, encapsulates the entire Pentateuch with all its power and glory, and with all its gifts and blessings. If you have the right consciousness, every time you recite the Genesis Prayer it'll be like reading the entire Pentateuch in its original form.

There's still much more concealed here, so much more. As we'll see in Part VI, the Genesis Prayer derives its essence from the primordial constant pi, and as pi converts any straight line into a circle, the Genesis Prayer thus bends in on itself to encircle us in its cleansing and protective light. As it encircles us in endless light, the **42**-letter Genesis Prayer forms a protective and incubating womb around us. As all the sages knew, it's no coincidence that the word "mother" has the value **42** and "womb" 248, or that the Torah is **42** rows deep and 248 columns wide.

DRAWING THE LIGHT INTO OUR WORLD

צית   שקו

Tav Yud Tsaddie   *Vav Koof Shin*   ←

Picture Your World as a Well and That All the Energy of All the Connections Made Above is Pouring Into It. Your Body Can Also Be a Well or Vessel for That Energy.

The 203 from **203**000 is even more telling; it's the same value as the word *Be'er,* "well," as in the wells where all the Patriarchs met their soul mates. According to the sages, a well is a code word for female receptive energy and a flowing of the life force, so it's most fitting that the word "well" was coded into the Genesis Prayer in the *Malckut* level, the level that receives all the flowing energy from the six other levels, which the sages tell us are masculine in aspect. The concept of well is also important because we can't drink from a well unless we do some physical action like pumping or hoisting up a bucket. And so it is with the seventh line and the *Malckut* or physical level, a well into which all the other levels (lines) deposit their energy.

❧

BREAKING THE CODE

The word *be'er* is found 22 times in the Pentateuch, yet another reference to the 22 Hebrew/Aramaic letters, which according to the sages are the physical manifestation of the 22 universal life forces.

❧

RENEWAL/STARTING AGIAN

שקוצית

Tav Yud Tsaddie Vav Koof Shin   ←

Meditate on Renewing All Your Relationships, Including with the Creator, to Start Again Fresh

As we meditate on this seventh line, and all six letters taken together instead of in pairs or triplets, we want to meditate on renewal, starting again. We can use this line specifically to jump-start any process in life that's stuck in the muck, whether it's our career, our love life, a project we're working on, or even a lifelong dream of ours. Like a TV screen that gets refreshed twelve times a second, we renew our relationships every second: with God and the universe (or the forces that be in the universe); with our loved ones, co-workers, employers and employees alike, our neighbors, and the community at large.

We all know how one offensive word can destroy those relationships instantly, or at least send them spiraling down the drain. They can all be lost with one lapse, in one split second. That's why, like the TV screens, we need to replenish our relationships so often. The truth, which is so hard for all of us to see when we're in the thick of an argument, is that those relationships can all be saved, can all be improved with one pleasant word. That's where this seventh line comes in: it gives us a boost, recharges us, helps replenish and refresh all our relationships; it helps get us a second chance, in a sense, forgiveness. Since none of us are saints, we *need* this constant refreshing, the more the better.

RECEIVING THE LIGHT

שקוציּת

Tav Yud Tsaddie Vav Koof Shin

Meditate to Absorb the Light/Energy into Your Body and Mind

Another purpose of this seventh line is to draw energy into our bodies and minds, to help make us one with the power of the Pentateuch. This seventh line completes the circuit, converting the Genesis Prayer into a handy wireless remote control for the Bible. The power of the Pentateuch is limitless; it's really a *universal* remote control for our lives. So far, man has barely tapped into the power and gifts of the Bible, but the Genesis Prayer is our opportunity; it opens the door—many doors. All we have to do is step through.

But like all doors, they swing both ways. With the wrong consciousness they close tight, locking us out, which is why the sages tell us the Genesis Prayer can do no harm. It's designed to stay with us as a protective shield while we go about our day, grabbing the fruits of the Tree of Life, but if we let anger swell up inside us, or if we get reactive at someone or some circumstance, then the doors shut tight behind us, thus prohibiting us from abusing this wonderful gift.

Fortunately, all we need to do is gather ourselves again, analyze where we were reactive, examine what pushed our buttons, and review what we can change about ourselves, and the gates will reappear, the doors will swing open again.

Because most of us can't control our reactivity, it's best to do the Genesis Prayer at least twice a day, though doing it even once puts you ahead of the game and gives you a big advantage over the rest of the world.

BREAKING THE CODE

Even the word "to receive," קבל *(Kahbel)*, is embedded into this line's meditation. The sages tell us that feminine energy is receptive energy and masculine is giving, like the positive and negative ends of an electric circuit, and thus we're also told that the first six lines of the Genesis Prayer are masculine in nature, allowing the energy to flow down through them, right into the seventh line, the feminine one, their receptacle, so to speak. The sages use the term their *vessel* or *chalice*. Moreover, since the Genesis Prayer is a microcosm of the Pentateuch, the Bible itself provides us with an excellent schematic for this design: Leah gave birth first to six boys and then one girl, representing the six upper masculine dimensions and *Malckut,* the feminine one, the one designed to receive.

THY KINGDOM COME;
THY WILL BE DONE ON EARTH
(BRINGING THE MESSIAH INTO OUR LIVES)

אבג יתצ
קרע שטנ
נגד יכש
בטר צתג
חקב טנע
יגל פזק
שקו צית

ש ק ו צ י ת

Tav Yud Tsaddie Vav Koof Shin

Visually Connect with All 42 Letters as a Whole, and While Looking at This Seventh Line, Meditate to Bring the Limitless Pure Consciousness of the Messiah into Your Life and Our World, the Entire World

This seventh level is associated with the lineage of the Messiah, which according to the sages stems from Jacob's son *Yehuda* (Judah), a man of action and tremendous power. Leah named him *Yehuda* because the word means "Thanks unto God." The lineage then flows on through to his descendant, another man of action and enormous power, King David, and then on to the Messiah, *Mashiach Ben David*. Amazingly, there are **42** *Yehuda's* in the Pentateuch, representing the **42** letters of the entire Genesis prayer that are all manifest in this seventh line. Moreover, concealed within Yehuda's (יהודה) name is the Tetragrammaton (יהוה), meaning we're connecting to **42** Tetragrammatons as well, one for each letter of the Genesis Prayer.

❧

BREAKING THE CODE

The added protection of *Yehuda* (Judah) and the Tetragrammaton is a powerful boost of energy in itself, but when we sum up the Pentateuch (Torah) occurrences of each of the six letters of this seventh line (ת,י,צ,ו,ק,ש), we get the number 104246, which is remarkable because as we've just explained, the **10** dimensions (*sefirot*) are represented in the last triplet of this line and more important because 424 is both the numerical value of the "Messiah, son of David" (*Mashiach Ben David*) and of the "Life Force" (*Chayot*). It's one of those two dozen or so numerical values that trigger an instant acknowledgment from the sages. Redundancy is the hallmark of the Bible and thus the eight root of 104246, or in mathematical shorthand $\sqrt[8]{104246} = 4.24$, once again 424, the Messiah, *Mashiach Ben David*.

42 is the value for the word *cheled*, meaning "this world," as in our world, which the sages tell us corresponds to this level—the

Malckut level. Thus the encrypted codes are indicating to us and the sages alike that both the Genesis Prayer and the Messiah are meant for us, for our world, and that it is through this seventh line where we can drawn upon the life force.

~

One last indication that all the cables tied to the letters of the alphabet and their associative energies are wrapped up into one giant electrical plug that we can tap into through this seventh line is that when we sum up the names of each of the 22 letters we get 4248, a powerful merging of 424 and 248, both of which are intimately associated with this seventh line. Interestingly enough, the number of Torah words, letters, and verses (79,975, 304,805, and 5,845 respectively) can be multiplied together to give 142,482,278,369,375, and since 14 is the value for David (דוד) and 22 is representative of the 22 letters whose sum of their names in *gematria* is 4248 and since 278 is the numerical value of the word "the *gematria*," it's pretty obvious this is a clue inciting us and the sages before us to look deeper.

~

A LIFE PRESERVER IN DESPERATE TIMES
שק

It's Best if You Visualize Yourself Donning Burlap Sackcloth and Grieving for Whatever It Is You're Lacking, but You Can Just Meditate on the Two Letters as Well

According to the *Book of Raziel,* if you ever, God forbid, find yourself in dire straits and are grieving about your situation, meditate with all your heart on the seventh line of the Genesis Prayer. Your prayers will be heard on high. Remember, this is not for emergencies— for those circumstances use the first line of the Prayer and seek professional help. This is for when you feel the world closing in around you and you're getting desperate, as it was for Miri, and as it felt for me when I was trapped in Palestine.

According to the *Book of Raziel,* when we're feeling that desperation, we want to assume the contriteness of a griever and meditate on the *shin koof* (שק) of שקוצית, asking for help. It tells us explicitly that your prayers will be answered. The book explains that the *shin koof* (שק) is the word for "sackcloth," which the ancients knew to wear when grieving. God forbid any of us are ever in that state, but if we do find ourselves there, thank God, we have a way out.

It works particularly well for money, as Zack found out. Zack had been looking for work for several months, and money was running out, but to make matters go from dire to desperate was that he and his wife had a newborn. Zack was answering ads and interviewing as much as he could, but anybody who's lost his job in the present economy knows how frustrating that experience can be. One morning, just after I showed him the *shin koof* (שק) connection, he decided to ask for help with the Genesis Prayer while scanning the executive want ads. Suddenly he spotted a job description that suited him perfectly. The ad directed him, and of course anyone else interested, to send his résumé to the Human Resources Department, and Zack was about to do it when he decided to call the company instead and track down whoever it was who was going to do the actual hiring. He did the Genesis Prayer again and called. Sure enough, he not only found out who was hiring, but was able to get his e-mail address as well. Zack immediately sent off his résumé by e-mail, circumventing a process that usually leads nowhere, and insuring he'd get a fair shake. The next day he did the Genesis Prayer again and called up to see if his résumé had been received, but there was no answer. Twenty minutes later Zack's phone rang, and his prospective employer called to chat and arrange an immediate interview. Bottom line, Zack got the job offer. Sure, it was Zack's credentials, charisma, and proactive actions that got him the job, but what sparked him to suddenly get proactive? And what made everything line up for him? Why did this process turn out differently from all the others he'd been through? Zack credits the Genesis Prayer, and so do I.

Other sages explain that when we pray we need to really feel the need for what we're praying; in other words, we need to create a vessel for the Light to fill. A halfhearted prayer is like trying to add milk to a full cup of coffee—all we get is a mess. As explained, this seventh or *Malckut* line is the spiritual vessel into which pours all the Light generated through the other six. The prayers we make here help determine how much we're going to receive. When we align our prayers with the proper meditations of the seven lines and ask for what we desire from the heart, as if grieving, as if we're impoverished and have nothing, the sages tell us our prayers will be answered, just like Zack's.

MONEY MATTERS

The first two letters of this line (שׁק) form the first two letters of *shekel,* the biblical word for money, and they add up to 400, as in the 400 shekels Abraham paid for the Cave of Machpelah, the place where most of the Patriarchs are buried, and thus this final line connects us once again to the energy and blessings of the Patriarchs and Matriarchs, and is also yet another reason that this two-letter meditation works so well with money issues—something far too many of us have.

BREAKING THE CODE

The first two letters of this line (שׁק), the final letter that anchors this seventh line (ת), and the four *Koofs* in the Genesis Prayer (ק) all have the value 400, as in the 400 shekels that Abraham paid for the Cave of Machpelah. According to the Arizal, because שׁק totals 400, this sequence and meditation also connects us to the holy linen of the High Priest and to the

400 worlds or 400 levels of holiness and also to the 4 *Yuds* of *Chochma,* which together total 400. The connection to linen is twofold: one, sackcloth was made of linen, and two, the word *sackcloth* in *gematria atbash* spells "linen." Thus this connection/meditation elevates us from our grief and negativity to holiness with the support of the Patriarchs.

THE MOST IMPORTANT CONNECTION OF ALL

שַׂקּוּ צִית

Meditate to Manifest All the Meditations You've Done so That They All Come Through for You, and Make a Resolution to Follow Through

Here's the most important connection of all. You don't have to do it every time. If you do it only once correctly you may never have to do another meditation again. The seventh line is special; it's different than the others, very different.

The seventh line is **CONCRETE POWER.** This line is *Malckut*; it's about manifestation, doing things. If the other lines are about space age, twenty-fifth-century technology, wireless communication, warp drives, hidden gates, and worm tunnels, this line is about steam shovels and bulldozers. Use it to burst through all the barriers and rip out all the fences.

Use this line with power and conviction; use it to tackle your worst problems first; blast them out of the way. The power is concrete, it's palpable, you can feel it, grab onto it, and hurl it at your enemies, but not those people you perceive to have it in for you. They're not your real enemies; they're actually your allies if you can get past the illusions. Our real enemies are the negativity we keep inside us, the self-destructive drive we all have that makes us cling to our indulgent nature like a child to pacifier. These are our dark secrets, the ones we share with no one, the ones that have been holding us back for so long.

Here is where we can grab hold of them with both hands and tear them out. Normally we can't see it, but the upper lines have weakened it, stunned it, and momentarily frozen it in our headlights. It's there all right. Rip it out and smash it to pieces. You've been energized, empowered, given special vision and powerful guides to help you, angels to lift your arms and guide your fists. It's up to you. Now's the opportunity! Seize it! Look inside, see whatever ugliness is there, and pull it out from the roots. Like tenacious weeds, they'll grow back if you don't get the roots. Don't leave them behind as a safety valve in case you change your mind at a later date. That's just doubts, and it's as good as pulling nothing out at all. You can't just say the words; you have to want to get them out. You've been gifted with certainty; show your appreciation and change. Visualize your negativity, your evil inclination; give it a name and pull it out from inside you. The upper dimensions are about potential: if you've done your meditations there, they've done the legwork for you; now it's about physicality; now it's about you putting in the effort.

Treat your negative inclination like the cancer it is; get every last bit of it. You'll know when you've succeeded.

BINDING OUR SOUL TO THE PENTATEUCH (TORAH)

יתצ	אבג
שטנ	קרע
יכש	נגד
צתג	במר
מנע	חקב
פזק	יגל
צית	שקו

A final word before we seal off and protect the connections. We know from the sages that the seven lines of the Genesis Prayer correspond to the seven dimensions *(sefirot),* and that both of them correspond to the seven words of the first verse of the Bible, Genesis 1:1, the seven words of creation. The sages also tell us that one of the most important steps in the ancient and traditional wedding ceremony is the circling of the groom by the bride seven times, because it binds their souls together according to the natural order of creation and the universe. As we recite the Genesis Prayer that stems directly from these seven words of the Bible's first verse, we, too, are binding our souls with the Pentateuch (Torah). According to the sages, the Pentateuch (Torah) is our bride. Reciting the Genesis Prayer performs the ceremony.

SEALING THE CONNECTION

We whisper this last line silently to ourselves:

(ברוך שם כבוד מלכותו לעולם ועד)

Va'ed L'olam Malckutoh Kevod Shem Baruch ← (whisper silently)

(Blessed is the Name of His Noble Kingdom forever and ever)

Regardless whether or not you attempted that final introspective workout, you'll receive enormous benefits from just doing the Genesis Prayer, but now we want to protect those benefits. It's like locking in the profits on a good stock trade. We need to close the deal and bank the profit, spiritual or otherwise. The final line of the Genesis Prayer is so powerful that it's recited silently in order to ground the connection, all the connections.

This line is like a ground wire—the third prong on electrical plugs—insuring us against short circuits. Technically, it's not part of the Genesis Prayer; it's a special phrase given to us by Jacob the Patriarch, and is said after many powerful connections to open us up to receive them and to seal them in. Then again, it is based on complex technology and when whispered silently after the seventh line it becomes an integral part of the whole prayer, expanding the power and reach of the Genesis Prayer by connecting it to the fully expanded Tetragrammaton, and by incorporating the twenty-four permutations of the Tetragrammaton (יהוה) through the twenty-four letters of the phrase.

The above explanations covered a lot of ground and connected us to powerful positive forces available to us in the universe, so it would be a good idea to review it from time to time in order to refresh our knowledge and strengthen our insights, but the simple version of the Genesis Prayer, the recommended one for our busy lives, as provided at the beginning of Part V, can be done in just a few minutes without any complicated explanations or any of the enhanced and/or supplemental meditations, such as are provided in Part V and in Appendixes Three and Four.

While the supplemental meditations are optional, they are recommended once you become familiar with the basic Genesis Prayer. They'll afford you additional control over your life and the universe around you.

Provided for your convenience in the next section are two summary meditations. The first is a short basic meditation sheet covering everything you need to do the Genesis Prayer and bring miracles into your life, and the second is a review of *all* the line-by-line meditations we covered in this section, everything you need to change your world.

PART V

ENHANCING
THE MEDITATION

16

Summary Basic Meditation

TRY A PRACTICE GENESIS PRAYER NOW AND SEE FOR YOUR-self how quick and easy it is. It'll help expand your consciousness before tackling Part VI and the supplemental meditations.

← *Read Transliteration from Right to Left*

<table>
<tr><td>צרור תתיר ימינך גדולת</td><td> בכח אנא</td><td>חסד</td><td>1 ←</td></tr>
<tr><td>urah Tatir   Yeminechah Gedulat</td><td>B'ko'ack Ana</td><td>(Chesed)</td><td>Line I</td></tr>
</table>

Meditate: **אבג יתצ** Unconditional love, replacing senseless hatred with human dignity for all. *Etz Ha'Cha'im,* the Tree of Life reality, connecting us to the spiritual realm where we have no limitations, where we can reach our true potentials and true fulfillment.

<table>
<tr><td>נור טהרנו שגבנו עמך</td><td>רנת קבל</td><td>(גבורה)</td><td>2 ←</td></tr>
<tr><td>rah Taharenu   Sagvenu Amechah</td><td>Rinat Kahbel</td><td>(Gevurah)</td><td>Line 2</td></tr>
</table>

Meditate: **קרע שטן** Literally *"kara satan,"* to tear out our evil in-clination from the seed level, letting go of all our doubts and neg-ativity. When we rearrange the letters we get *"sha'ar katan,"* small gates; we want to close these gates and not let in the darkness and doubts in the first place. It's the same value as the world *tishkack,* to forget; we want to forget the limitations we impose on ourselves by calculating, by using our egos instead of letting the Light do the thinking for us. We want to forget the limitations and illusions of physicality, like time and space. They're not obstacles for us.

כבבת שמרם   דור שי יחודך   נא גבור   (תפארת)   3

Shomrem Kevavat   Yichudechah Dorshay   Gibor Na   (*Tiferet*)   Lin

Meditate: **נגד יכש,** *nun gimmel dalet,* for sustenance through sharing and tithing, a partnership with the Light of the Creator. Use the *Yud Caf Shin* as a spiritual *mikve* for removing all our negativity and rejuvenating and replacing the sparks we lost to the *klippot,* to our dark side.

תמיד גמלם   רחמי צדקתך   ברכם טהרם   (נצח)   4

Gomlem Tamid   Tsidkatechah Rackamay   Taharem Barckem   (*Netzach*)   Lir

Meditate: **בטר צתג** This line gives us the power of perseverance, the willpower to succeed.

נהל עדתך   ברוב טובך   חסין קדוש   (הוד)   5

Adatechah Nahel   Tuvchah Berov   Kadosh Khasin   (*Hod*)   Lir

Meditate: **חקב טנע** This line gives us the power of deep insight, and overcoming temptations.

זוכרי קדושתך   לעמך פנה   יחיד גאה   (יסוד)   6

K'dushatechah Zocrey   P'nay L'amcha   Geh'eh Yackid   (*Yesod*)   Lir

Meditate: **יגל פזק** This sequence helps us to reveal the secrets of the sages and the Bible for the whole planet, ushering in the Messiah

(Mashiach) consciousness in this the sixth millennium, spreading the wisdom of the Genesis Prayer to the entire world.

← 7	(מלכות)	שׁוּעתנוּ קבּל	וּשׁמע צעקתנוּ	יוֹדע תעלוּמוֹ
Line 7	*(Malckut)*	Kahbel Shavatenu	Tsa'akatenu Ushma	'alumot Yodea

Meditate: שׁקוּ צית This line is for renewal, starting again, manifesting all the connections.

(בּרוּך שׁם כּבוֹד מלכוּתוֹ לעוֹלם וער)

(Va'ed L'olam Malckutoh Kevod Shem Baruch) ← (whisper silently)

Whisper the last line silently to ground the connection and build our vessel.

This first time it probably took you around four minutes to complete the meditation; after all, the transliterated words are unfamiliarly read from right to left and are very difficult to pronounce, but with a little practice you'll be able to reduce that by half. What's two minutes toward a lifetime of miracles and fulfillment for you and your family!

We've provided a complete pure *Ana B'ko'ack*/Genesis Prayer meditation in Appendix One for your convenience. It incorporates some of the enhanced meditative qualities discussed in the next section, and in this complete pure state it is visually much more powerful for us and our connections. This purer version includes all the vowels and *tagins,* special flourishes crowning the letters, which if you can't read Hebrew won't mean much to you, but visually they add additional levels of energy that we all can use. It's important, though, to use the Summary Meditations in this section until you're familiar enough with the process, eventually switching to the purer version in Appendix One when ready. To further assist us in the meditative process, we've included a complete summary of *all* the meditations, which you can refer to at any time for easy reference. Remember, we can always refer back to the text and the written-out meditations and explanations at any time. I do.

SUMMARY REVIEW OF ALL THE LINE-BY-LINE MEDITATIONS

Line 1

Chesed/Mercy/Abraham

Tsrurah Tatir	Yeminechah Gedulat	B'ko'ack Ana	(*Chesed*)	1
תתיר צרורה	**גדולת ימינך**	**אנא בכח**	**(חסד)**	1

	יתצ		**אבג**	
	Tsaddie, Tav, Yud		Gimmel, Bet, Alef	←

אבג יתצ Connect to Abraham, the Father of spirituality, and our Father in Heaven.

אבג יתצ Connect to and wrap yourself in the energy of the entire Pentateuch (Torah).

אבג יתצ Meditate on feeling and sharing unconditional love for the whole world.

אנא Meditate on bathing and cleansing yourself inside and out with spiritual water or Light.

אבג יתצ Dissolve the world around you until you find yourself in the spiritual realm, where there are no limitations.

Line 2

Gevurah/Strength and Judgment/Isaac

Norah Taharenu	Sagvenu Amechah	Rinat Kahbel	(*Gevurah*)	2
טהרנו נורא	**עמך שגבנו**	**קבל רנת**	**(גבורה)**	2

	שטנ		**קרע**	
	Nun Tet Shin		Ayin Resh Koof	←

קרע שטנ	Meditate to cut out your negative inclinations.
קרע שטנ	Let go of your selfish desires.
שער קטנ	Meditate to not be influenced by the negativity of others, and ask for strength against provocations.
קרע שטנ	Ask for the strength to get out of your comfort zone and to go the extra mile.
שטנ and קרע	Meditate to take your ego and personal agendas out of your dealings, and to stop calculating and second-guessing your good intentions.
קרע שטנ	Suspend your disbelief and go with the flow. Meditate to keep the gates of certainty open.
קרע שטנ	Meditate on a specific situation you want changed and what outcome you'd like to see.

Line 3

Tiferet/Beauty/Jacob

omrem Kevavat	Yichudechah Dorshay	Gibor Na	(*Tiferet*)	3 ←
כבבת שמ	דורשי יחודך	נא גבור	(תפארת)	3 ←

	יכש	נגד
	Shin Caf Yud	Dalet Gimmel Nun	←

נגד	Meditate to receive sustenance through sharing and/or tithing, or to form a partnership with the universe.
יכש	Ask that your sins and negative thoughts and deeds get purged at the seed level from your psychological, emotional, physical, and spiritual states.
יכש	Meditate on this sequence entering your body as a pinprick of bright white light, chasing out any darkness harbored inside, then envision the light spreading rapidly from cell to cell, organ to organ, until your whole body is glowing bright white and all the negativity has dissipated into the atmosphere, leaving you in perfect health. Repeat

on others you care about, and on your community as a whole, then on any trouble spots in the world, such as the Mideast.

שדי   Meditate that this Name of God stays with you all day and is at the entrance to all your dealings, and ask that it protect you from any negative forces.

נגכ שדי   Meditate that you connect with the Archangel Metatron and ask for any knowledge that can help you in your spiritual quest.

Line 4

Netzach/Victory/Moses

Gomlem Tamid	Tsidkatechah Rackamay	Taharem Barckem	*Netzach*	4
תמיד גמלם	רחמי צדקתך	ברכם טהרם	(נצח)	4
	צתג	בטר		
	Gimmel Tav Tsaddie	Resh Tet Bet		←

רצ   Meditate that you've traveled through a cosmic gateway and are at the Well of Miriam. You want to sip from the water and ask to meet your soul mate, not just your marriage one, but the others with whom you should do business, have friendships, and so on.

רצ   List your spiritual desires or concentrate on one of them and ask that they (it) be fulfilled.

רצ   Meditate to strengthen your relationships, including with humanity, to help draw in your soul mates.

רצ   Meditate that you're at the Well of Miriam and that you want your spouse to have a healthy child or to conceive, as the case may be. Even more powerful is to meditate that everyone who wants to conceive gets to.

בטר צתג   Ask for the willpower and perseverance to see things through to victory, to achieve your goals, especially the ones you set at the outset of the Genesis Prayer.

במר צתג   Meditate to receive the will to succeed, to get the Olympian spirit, and to see past the obstacles.

Line 5

Hod/Splendor/Aaron

Natechah Nahel	Tuvchah Berov	Kadosh Khasin	*Hod*	5 ←
נחל עדר	ברוב טובך	חסין קדוש	(הוד)	5 ←
	טנע	חקב		
	Ayin Nun Tet	Bet Koof Chet		

חק   Meditate to connect to and elevate our consciousness to that of Sarah, Rebecca, Leah, and Rachel and to Enoch in order to see things at a higher level, intuitively and prophetically.

חקב   Ask that you receive prophetic dreams through the merits of Jacob and Yosef. This is another opportunity to ask for miracles.

חקב טנע   Meditate to be able to draw upon the divine inspiration stored up in this cosmic level.

חקב טנע   Ask to be able to see and comprehend the signs that are all around you and to receive the inspiration to make the "right" choices in life.

חק   Ask that Sarah, Rebecca, Leah, and Rachel help you to see past the illusions and temptations that cause you to make the wrong decisions in life.

Line 6

Yesod/Foundation/Yosef

ushatechah Zockray	P'nay L'amcha	Geh'eh Yackid	*Yesod*	6 ←
זוכרי קדושו	לעמך פנה	יחיד גאה	(יסוד)	6 ←
	פזק	יגל		
	Koof Zayin Pe	Lamed Gimmel Yud		←

לפ

Ask Yosef to be your conduit for drawing down the miracles you've previously requested and any others that you may need but are unaware of.

יגל פזק

Make yourself a channel for spreading the wisdom of the Genesis Prayer to the whole world by meditating on everyone receiving it and on what actions you can take to share it with others.

יגל פזק

Meditate on peace/human dignity/Messiah consciousness for all.

Line 7

Malckut/Kingdom/Manifestation/King David and the Messiah

Ta'alumot Yode'ah	Tsa'akatenu Ushma	Kahbel Shavatenu	*Malckut*
יודע תעלומות	ושמע צעקתנו	שועתנו קבל	(מלכות)
	צית	שקו	
	Tav Yud Tsaddie	Vav Koof Shin	←

יתצ - צית

Meditate that the Genesis Prayer is the House of God, a House of Light, and that you're in it.

שקו צית

See the Genesis Prayer superimposed on an open Torah scroll made of white light and then see yourself wrapped up in it like a warm blanket of white light, a cocoon of bright white Light.

שקו צית

Meditate to draw in the Eternal Light, by visualizing yourself in the Holy Temple in Jerusalem, aglow in the Light that comes from the time of creation and extends through you out toward eternity.

שקו צית

Picture your world as a well and that all the energy of all the connections made above is pouring into it. Your body can also be a well or vessel for that energy.

שקו צית

Meditate on renewing all your relationships, including with the Creator, to start again fresh.

שקוצית

Meditate to absorb the Light/energy into your body and mind.

ש ק ו צ י ת   Visually connect with all 42 letters as a whole, and while looking at this seventh line, meditate to bring the limitless pure consciousness of the Messiah into your life and our world, the entire world.

שק   It's best if you visualize yourself donning burlap sackcloth and grieving for whatever it is you're lacking, but you can just meditate on the two letters as well.

שקו צית   Meditate to manifest all the meditations you've done so that they all come through for you, and make a resolution to follow through.

The Full 42 Letter Name and Meditation

אבג יתצ
קרע שטנ
נגד יכש
בטר צתג
חקב טנע
יגל פזק
שקו צית

(Va'ed L'olam Malckutoh Kevod Shem Baruch)   ← (whisper silently)

Meditate that this line grounds the connection for you and builds your vessel.

17

Enhanced Meditations

THE GENESIS PRAYER IS NOTHING NEW; IN FACT, IT'S OLDER than the Bible. Who first did it is hard to say. Some sages say Adam and Enoch did it. What we know for sure is that Abraham did it and that he added an incredibly powerful aspect to it, the ability to tap into and harness the astrological forces of our universe. In his book the *Sefer Yetzirah,* or *Book of Formation,* he outlined specific letters that act as conduits to the energy of specific planets and others that connect to specific constellations and regions of the cosmic sky. Then, by pairing them up, he gave us the ability to take control of the astrological energy of the month and thus of our lives. The technology he used is beyond me, but from what I've seen of other technology he used and the secrets he revealed elsewhere in the book, secrets that led to the deciphering of the underlying codes of the Bible and of the Genesis Prayer, I have no reason to doubt him, and when it comes to astrology I come as a skeptic.

I'd always thought of astrology as small talk and 1970s pickup lines, but I have to admit, as of late I've found great insight into myself through kabbalistic astrology and have seen amazing predictions come true for people. Nevertheless, I know the depth of the technology and integration of the Genesis Prayer, and that it has invisible fibers stretching to the far corners of dimensions we can't even comprehend. If our modern physicists are correct and everything in our universe, physical and metaphysical, is connected by strings of energy also operating on a level beyond our comprehension, then why wouldn't Abraham also be correct about this? Why wouldn't specific letters have the innate ability to control the energy of entire quadrants of the universe?

I give him the benefit of the doubt, especially since I know that when I say the Genesis Prayer with the meditation for the correct letters of the month at the appropriate line, as in the chart on page 184, its results are much stronger.

Whether you believe in astrology or not, a few more extra seconds spent with the astrologically appropriate letters will improve your chances of removing stress from your life and reaching fulfilling goals. As always, the choice is yours.

The letters and connections are arranged in order of the lines of the Genesis Prayer with which they correspond, and the months correspond to Abraham's original calendar, which aligns somewhat with our astrological one but shifts from year to year. Feel free to use either the Hebrew calendar dates or the Western Astrological one to determine which is the appropriate zodiac line to use.

All we have to do to enhance our connections is insert a quick meditation on the two Hebrew/Aramaic letters at the end of their corresponding line of the Genesis Prayer and invoke the simple consciousness connection provided beneath the letters. In other words, go to the line that corresponds to the month we're in, and when you finish your normal Genesis Prayer meditations for that particular line you'll add this quick connection to help smooth out the wrinkles of the month. Referring to the chart provided on the next page, what you do is to meditate on the letter on the right that rules the Sign of the Month and on the letter on the left that rules the Planet of the Month, and then meditate that the letters are helping you fulfill the corresponding connections below them.

To make it even easier, we've superimposed the letters with their corresponding lines on the complete Genesis Prayer chart in Appendix One. The timing of the Hebrew months vis-à-vis our western calendar varies from year to year because the Hebrew calendar is based on a lunar calendar, but if we don't know what the Hebrew month is we can still use our Western months, which are based on the solar calendar, as guides.

Aramaic Letters

	Planet	Sign	Hebrew Month	Western Calend
	Saturn	Aquarius	Shevat	Jan 21—Feb 20
Line 1	(bet) צ ב	(tsaddie)		

We're going above all the natural limitations.

Line 1	Saturn	Capricorn	Tevet	Dec 22—Jan 19
	(bet) ע ב	(ayin)		

We want to connect to the energy of mind over matter, that of the עב, or 72 Names, i we have them.

Line 2	Jupiter	Pisces	Adar	Feb 19—March
	(gimmel) ק ג	(koof)		

We're connecting to joy, happiness, and miracles.

Line 2	Jupiter	Sagittarius	Kislev	Nov 22—Dec 2
	(gimmel) ס ג	(samech)		

Binah consciousness, the consciousness of understanding, and bringing down miracle and wonders into our lives.

	Sign	Planet	Hebrew Month	Western Calend
Line 3	Scorpio	Mars	Mar Cheshvan	Oct 24—Nov 2
	(nun) ד נ	(dalet)	(*Note:* The planet and sign placemen reverse here)	

We're connecting to the positive sharing aspect of all the water in the world, helping it return to its primordial state of grace before the flood, removing anger and jealousy from our lives. Meditate to convert *Mar Cheshvan* to *Ram Cheshvan,* changing *bitter* to *sweet* and thus sweetening the waters with mercy.

		Sign	Hebrew Month	Western Calendar
..e 3	Aries	Mars	Nissan	March 21—April 19
	(hei) ה ד *(dalet)*			

..e want to go to war against our own negativity, against our personal agendas.

| ..e 4 | Leo | Sun | Av | July 23—Aug 22 |
| | *(tet)* ט כ *(caf)* | | | |

..'re taking control of our ego by letting go.

| ..e 5 | Libra | Venus | Tishrei | Sept 23—Oct 23 |
| | *(lamed)* ל פ *(pay)* | | | |

..'re drawing energy from *Binah,* the cosmic energy store, and connecting to the *Bet* (ב)
..cealed within the *Pay* for the hidden blessings concealed within life.

| ..e 5 | Taurus | Venus | Iyar | April 20—May 20 |
| | *(vav)* ו פ *(pay)* | | | |

..'re connecting to the energy of healing and the hidden blessings in life.

| ..e 6 | Virgo | Mercury | Elul | Aug 23—Sept 22 |
| | *(yud)* י ר *(resh)* | | | |

..'re connecting to the energy of repentance, going back in time and undoing any
..ngs we've committed.

| ..e 6 | Gemini | Mercury | Sivan | May 21—June 21 |
| | *(zayin)* ז ר *(resh)* | | | |

..h and *Zayin* spell *raz,* "secret," also "Light." We can connect with immortality of all types.

	Planet	Sign	Hebrew Month	Western Calendar
..e 7	Moon	Cancer	Tammuz	June 22—July 22
	(tav) ת ח *(chet)*		(*Note:* The planet and sign placement reverse here.)	

We meditate to remove our anger and thus cancer from our lives at the
seed level.

PART VI

BREAKING THE CODES

18

In the Beginning . . .

IT'S SAID THAT THERE ARE MORE SECRETS AND GIFTS IN THE Bible than in Heaven and Earth—a paradox, but only if we limit ourselves to physicality.

> In the beginning of God's creation of heaven and earth, the earth was without form and empty. (Genesis 1:1)

As is fitting, the first verse of the Bible hints that God is above heaven and earth and thus his secrets would be, too. But to extend that metaphysical property to the Bible we'd have to believe it was created by God and not by a series of historians and storytellers, as is ever more commonly thought today. Why not? If we only take the Bible literally and don't look beneath the surface to all the underlying codes and the spiritual teachings, we might be tempted to think so, too; after all, there are many apparent inconsistencies, such as a commandment to the Israelites not to kill and then a call to slaughter their enemies. Without knowing that the names of those enemies have the same numerical value as the word "doubts" and without viewing those enemies as spiritual enemies, like doubts and egos, the Bible might not make sense to us, either. Nevertheless, let's suspend our disbelief for a moment and ask what it would mean if, as the sages believed, the Pentateuch (Torah) was written by God; if every letter, word, and verse held hidden meanings, blessings, and gifts; if every letter held such specific significance that it could not be changed or altered in any way without disrupting the absolute perfect fractal balance of the entire document? What would it mean if even today in the twenty-first century man couldn't have written such a document, let alone thirty-four hundred years ago when there were no computers, calculators, calculus, or even pads and pens?

It's far beyond the scope of this simple book to supply a proof of the questions posed above, and even though the sages have piled up tons of evidentiary proof, until we put it in strict and very boring mathematical terms, skeptics will still say that it's just coincidence, albeit over four hundred thousand of them. All that math and numbers would distract immeasurably from the purpose of this book, which is to bring miracles to as many people as possible through the Genesis Prayer. To the disappointed, we promise to tackle those questions posed above and bring all that evidentiary proof to light in subsequent books. Nevertheless, we did promise to show where the Genesis Prayer came from, and from that you should be able to glean some of the magnificence that went into the Pentateuch (Torah) itself.

THE GENESIS PRAYER: COSMIC NEXUS

Why all the math and numbers? One reason is that it's the only way for us to prove to ourselves concretely a Creator's and the Bible's validity. Another is that the numbers represent energy, giving us a code with which to unlock the energy gates of the universe, the ones that Abraham told us about. As our scientists tell us, all energy flows, transfers information, generates Light, and supports life. Once we open these gates we can tap them, tap into these endless sources of abundance. Abraham couldn't tell us where to find those gates in the Bible, because it didn't physically exist in his time, but he did give us the clues and the tools that we'd need. One of them is *gematria*; it acts as a blueprint to the Bible, showing us what type of energy is found where, and just as important, how to harness it.

Together, the numbers, equations, and *gematria* ciphers are the programming code that creates the software, while the prayers, meditations, and blessings are the software themselves. And like the software on our computers, they make our lives easier; all it takes is a little knowledge, patience, and practice. But just like computer software, it's not free; we have to earn it. In the case of the hidden Bible software, we have to earn it with our consciousness.

Who knows? Perhaps man wasn't ready before. Maybe it wasn't the right time. But we're ready now. We know this because it's available to us now. An omniscient force doesn't make mistakes; everything happens for a reason.

The very first equations in the Pentateuch spill out from its first verse, and they all come together to create the Genesis Prayer:

> In the beginning of God's creation of heaven and earth,
> the earth was without form and empty . . . (Genesis 1:1)

We have to use the original Hebrew/Aramaic and the *gematria* ciphers to get to the codes and the resultant software, but because simple math is straightforward and unambiguous, so are the conclusions. Here is the same verse as originally written:

בראשית ברא אלהים את השמים ואת הארץ:
והארץ היתה תהו וב ←

Because most of us don't read Hebrew/Aramaic, we'll get right into some of the underlying codes and how they relate to creation and the Genesis Prayer. Many scholars have done a great job describing the workings of *gematria,* and still others have touched on the spiritual significance of this passage, so there's no reason to get bogged down here when all we really want to do is get to the heart of the Genesis Prayer. In the same way that it's hard to say who first started using the Hebrew alphabet, or even numbers, we don't know when people started using *gematria,* although by all indications they happened simultaneously, as if a lightbulb went on in our consciousness.

There are several ways to apply *gematria* to this verse, and the most basic one is to sum up the standard *gematria* valuation for each letter, word by word, giving us 913, 203, 86, 401, 395, 407, and 296 for the first seven that make up the all-important first verse of the Bible and 302, 420, 411, and 8 for the rest of the words that complete the Bible's first **42** letters, which correspond to the **42** letters of the Genesis Prayer. To understand how deep the connection is between the Genesis Prayer and the Bible's first verse and creation—a time before the existence of time—we need to note that the sum of the first verse's **28** letters, or alternatively its 7 words, is 2701, exactly the same as the precise sum of all the integers from 1 to 73. Even the number 28 is the sum of the integers from 1 to 7.

We know from the sages and from our discussion of the Genesis Prayer's third line that 73 is the value associated with *Chochma,* the highest level next to God, the level of wisdom. And as the great sage R. Isaac Luria told us *Chochma* is the source from which all holiness spreads, we can see that the first verse was designed for us to climb all the energy levels from 1 to 73 and get next to God.

~

BREAKING THE CODE

While our scientists tell us that the sum of these 73 integers also satisfies the equation for $n = 73$, $(n^2 - n)/2 + n = 2701$, an even more complex mathematical relationship is found built into the seven words of the first verse. It lies in the sum of the first seven factorials: $\Sigma(1! - 7!) = (7 \times 6 \times 5 \times 4 \times 3 \times 2 \times 1) + (6 \times 5 \times 4 \times 3 \times 2 \times 1) + \cdots = 5913$. Five can represent the 5 Books, and 913 *is* the value of the first word in the verse, and because 5913 is evenly divisible by 73, yielding $5913/73 = 3^4$, representative of the perfect harmony of the balanced 3-column system and the 4 letters of the Tetragrammaton, we can see the complexity of thought that went into choosing the appropriate letters for this verse. But just in case we think this is all a coincidence, we should further note that according to the Bible and the sages who study it, the Israelites arrived at Mt. Sinai on **5/9/13**13 B.C.E.

There's much we know from the sages regarding this verse and its power, but what's clear is that since numbers represent potential energy levels with their inherent powers, there's obviously enormous power in all **73** of those numbers wrapped into one, just as it was in all those lines and columns of the Genesis Prayer, which each summed to 903, the sum of all the integers through **42**.

THE ALPHA CONSTANT

One simple link between the Genesis Prayer, the number 73, and the Bible's first verse is found in that 73 percent of the total value of the Genesis Prayer, or $(3701 \times .73)$, is exactly 2701.73, the total value of the Bible's first verse (2701), and 173 is the small *gematria* value of the **42** letters of the Genesis Prayer. Incidentally, when we divide the sum of the values in the Genesis Prayer by that of the Bible's first verse, we get $3701/2701 = 1.3702$, and not only is 137 the value of *kabbalah*, meaning "to receive," and 702 the value of *Sabbath*, but 1/137.0 is the value of the alpha or fine structure constant, the measure of the strength of the electromagnetic force that governs how electrically charged particles such as electrons interact with light photons. So what we're receiving is wisdom (73, *Chochma*), possibly the wisdom of the ages, because most astrophysicists agree today that the age of the universe is 13.7 billion years old, the same as the largest known object in the universe, 1.37 light years across. This may all be coincidence, but what it's not is manipulation—these numbers are all immutable. Even Richard Feynman, one of the greatest minds of the twentieth century, says, "[the Alpha Constant, $1/137.03\ldots$] is one of the greatest damn mysteries of physics: a magic number that comes to us with no understanding by man," and "the hand of G-d wrote that number, and we don't know how He pushed his pencil."

~

As a mathematician, I found myself in the skeptic category, but I was hard pressed to come up with alternative solutions, and thus couldn't ignore the numbers. This couldn't be an accident. Not many people would argue that at this point. But staring face to face with the Torah, which I'm finding to be such an awe-inspiring work of art and science, I have to remind myself that the numbers are just codes; the real purpose of them is to highlight their spiritual underpinnings.

~

THE FIRST NAME OF GOD

We've already seen how the Genesis Prayer was designed to emulate and synchronize with the Pentateuch (Torah) and how the number of the occurrences of the fourth, second, and fifth words of the Bible's first verse is also 2701, and how the 228 (the value of the word *blessed*) occurrences of the verse's third word, *Elohim*, God, sums with its word value 86 to create 314, whose significance as Metatron and pi will be obvious momentarily. But yet another mathematically fantastic aspect about the Name *Elohim* (אלהים) is that its five letters can be divided into three consecutive triplets (אלה להי הים), and they each sum numerically to the exact sum of all the integers through the consecutive integers 8, 9, and 10, for a total of 36, 45, and 55 respectively. Since these perfect sums of integers can be arranged in pyramid form to create perfect equilateral triangles, they are also called triangular numbers. Interestingly enough, the twenty-two letters of the Hebrew/Aramaic alphabet can be arranged into 22^5 or 5,153,632 different combinations of possible five-letter words, and of them all only the combination *Elohim* (אלהים), the third word in the Bible, meets this criteria of forming three consecutive triangular triplets. Moreover, the sum of those three triangular numbers (36, 45, 55) plus the *kolel* is 137, and in small gematria, the sum of the three triplets is 1,000.

~

That the first Name of God in the Bible is unique and forms three consecutive triangular triplets is not surprising if we know that both the twenty-eight letters of the first verse and the value of that verse, 2701, can be likewise arranged into perfect equilateral triangles. The value 2701 forms a perfect equilateral triangle with 73 rows and a perimeter triangle of 216, or $6 \times 6 \times 6$, while the 28 letters form a perfect triangle of 7 rows with a perimeter triangle of 18, or $6 + 6 + 6$.

~

I find myself wondering how anyone thirty-eight hundred years ago could have kept track of all those words and letter sequences. After all, the law was that any mistake in the Torah invalidates it, and that if a mistake was found the entire page had to be rewritten. Additionally, each time a scribe writes the Name of God—and there are thousands of them in the Torah—he has to take a *mikve* first. How many lifetimes would a trial-and-error approach have taken to write the Torah? Beyond that, whoever created the Torah would also have had to design most of the key words in it from scratch, let alone choose which ones to put where and how many of each one were mathematically necessary. If this huge combinatorial jigsaw puzzle were only numbers, and not words with distinct and sometimes subtle meanings, the challenge would be great enough, but without a computer I don't know how they could have done that.

When we examined the meditations of the third line of the Genesis Prayer we discussed how 314 and 73 were numerically integrated into that line and how they were a gateway to Metatron and to the highest level of wisdom and knowledge, *Chochma*. We'll see in a moment how these two numbers, and what they represent, are also even more integrally connected to the Bible's first verse, and how 314 is unambiguously the value of pi, which wasn't supposed to have been known back then but, as we'll soon see, was repeatedly integrated into the Pentateuch's design to at least six decimal places.

In order to comprehend the grand complexity built into the first verse, let's first examine the significance of it having 28 letters. It must be a very important number, because there are literally hundreds of statistically impossible instances of 28 occurring naturally in the Pentateuch (Torah), a sampling of which is in the box below. More germane to our purpose is that the influence of the powerful number 28, as we've explained, is represented twice in the Bible's first verse. Moreover, we know from the sages that the numerical value 28 has multiple significant meanings, including "power," "By God," "union with God," "together," "collectivity," "union," and "unity."

~~

THE NUMBER 28

Here's a sampling of how the entire Pentateuch (Torah) revolves around the key number 28: The square root of the number of words (79,976) in the Torah is 282.8002828; those words divided by 28 (79,976/28) = 2856.28; the amount of numbers in the Chronicles of Adam is 28; the number of *heys* (ה)—the fifth letter in the Hebrew/Aramaic alphabet—in the Five Books of Moses is 28,056, while the sum of the five final letters in the Hebrew/Aramaic alphabet, the ones with special properties, is 280; and just in case we were to think the 28,056 *heys* and their value of 140,280 is a coincidence, there are exactly 90,100 *yuds* (י), *heys* (ה), and *vavs* (ו) in the Torah, which can combine to construct exactly 14,028 Tetragrammatons (יהוה); moreover, the value for the word "The *Torah*" (616) divided by the 22 letters that comprise it (616/22) = 28; and the Matriarchs Sarah and Leah are each mentioned 28 times, while the value for *Yehoshua* (Joshua, salvation, "the Throne of Mercy," and probably Jesus, 391) is also found 28 times; while there are only 5 numbers found exactly 28 times, the number 28 is the 26th word value present in the Pentateuch, as in the value of the Tetragrammaton (26); and the value of the 7,032 *dalets* (ד) in the Torah = 28128; finally, since the total valuation of all 304,805 letters in the Torah is 21,009,826, it too connects to 28 in that the sum of all the digits in 21,009,826 is $(2 + 1 + 0 + 0 + 9 + 8 + 2 + 6) = 28$ and the product of them $(2 \times 1 \times 9 \times 8 \times 2 \times 6)$ is 1728, but an even bigger surprise is found when we use a deeply revealing form of *gematria* to get $\sqrt[4]{(P_{(21009826)}/\sum_{(21009826)})}$ or $\sqrt[4]{(1728/28)} = 2.802828$.

~

BREAKING THE CODE

There is some dispute as to the spelling of Jesus's Hebrew name, though in all probability it is the same as that of Joshua, יהושע, which combines *Yah* (יה), a high Name of God that the sages tell us is associated with creation, and ושע, which has the same value as 376 (*shalom*, peace) and a reference to the Hebrew year 3760, when Jesus was born (0 C.E.). 391 is also the value of the phrase "Throne of God," which the sages tell us is connected to the third line of the Genesis Prayer.

~

THE TETRAGRAMMATON

Astonishingly, those 90,100 *yuds* (י), *heys* (ה), and *vavs* (ו) in the Torah also represent a connection to the Messiah because 90,100 is the sum of the integers ($\sum 1$–424), and as stated earlier, 424 is the value of *Mashiach Ben David*, the Messiah.

~

THE CREATION EQUATION:
3.14159265358 . . .

> In the beginning of God's creation of heaven and earth,
> the earth was without form and empty. (Genesis 1:1)

We'll get to how 3, pi, the Genesis Prayer, and the Bible's first verse integrate and link both the Genesis Prayer and Genesis itself to creation, but first there is another link between pi and Genesis's first verse that we'd like to establish. As detailed in the box below, the values of the twenty-eight letters juxtaposed with those of the seven words is equivalent to the actual value of pi to five decimal places, a very close approximation to pi, but we'll see some much closer ones in a moment.

PI TO FIVE DECIMAL PLACES

A cursory review of the **7** words, comprised of **28** letters, that make up the Pentateuch's first verse reveal that they spell out a very interesting equation. First we take the number of letters (**28**) and divide them by the number of words (**7**), giving us 28/7 or 4, which we know is always representative of the four letters of the Tetragrammaton (יהו׳ה). But when we multiply 28/7 by the product (multiple) of the numerical value of each of the **28** letters, and then divide that by the value of the product of the values of the **7** words, we get **pi**:

$$(28 \text{ letters}/7 \text{ words}) \times (P_{gematria}(28 \text{ letters})/P_{gematria}(7 \text{ Words}))$$
$$= 3.141545078 \times 10^{-07}$$
$$= (28/7) \times (23887872000/30415352578 \times 10^{17})$$
$$= 3.141545078$$

The rather large division of the two *gematria* products yields 3.14155, a variance from true pi of only .0012142 percent. It works out the same whether we use small *gematria* or standard *gematria;* just the decimal place changes, an important concept based on what we're about to see.

≈

To the sages, who already had certainty in the divine providence of the Torah and Creation, this equation indicated that we could use this verse to connect directly to the wisdom of God. To them, it wasn't numbers, but a reflection of the Tetragrammaton multiplied by the full energy of the "power" of creation juxtaposed with the full channel between our physical world and the metaphysical one. When these juxtapositions are properly aligned, the wisdom flows right to us unencumbered; that's what the Genesis Prayer is for. It acts as our interface and helps align our consciousness with the energies of the universe.

Before we examine other creation equations, let's take a moment to examine pi itself (3.14159265358 . . .) and see why it's being used so extensively by the Bible and by the sages—why it's considered a gateway to the Ultimate Wisdom. Pi is a supposedly random and infinite sequence of numbers that happens to govern the curvature of a straight line into a circle, and needless to say, this is no man-made concept. Pi necessarily had to come into existence at the first moment of creation, thus stretching back to the dawn of time. Man *may* have written the Torah, but he played no part in creation or pi. No one will argue this. Nonetheless, before we get into these closer approximations to pi and the deeper links to Genesis and the Genesis Prayer, let's examine the numeric relationship between 314 and 358, the "Messiah," as they appear within the first 10 digits of pi.

The ten-dimensional structure to our universe was first described by Abraham thirty-eight hundred years ago in the *Sefer Yetzirah,* or *Book of Formation,* but about fifteen years ago the ten-dimensional structure suddenly became popular and was swiftly adopted by modern physicists. They called it a superstring theory. Today, it's almost universally accepted that our greater universe has ten dimensions.[4] The sages often said, "As above, so it is below," and so it is that all our basic mathematics and counting systems are based on the base-10 numbering system.

If 10 represents the highest level of the 10 dimensions *(sefirot),* then finding 358, the value for *Mashiach,* the Messiah, at the 10th digit in pi, (3.14159265**358** . . .) must mean something. Of course, the first 3 digits in pi (**3.14**159265358 . . .) numerically spell out 314, which is the value of *Shaddai,* the Almighty, and also of the highest Archangel, Metatron.

～

GOD IN PI

Interesting enough, the Name *Shaddai* (שדי), the "Almighty," is found **10** times in the Torah, and the sum of the digits between **314** (*Shaddai*) and **358** (the Messiah) within pi is **28**, as in the first verse's **28** letters. Other Names of God numerically encoded within these **10** digits of Pi, include **31, 41, 15, 26,** and **65. 31** (*El,* אל) is the first two digits (**3.1**4159265358); **41** numerically spells "*Yah,* the Lord (יהיה יי) and it is the number of letters in the spelled out highest Name of God, *Ehyeh* (אהיה), (3.14**15**9265358); **15** numerically spells *Yah* (יה) (3.14**15**926 5358); and then comes **26,** the Tetragrammaton (יהוה) (3.14 159**26**5358) attached to **65** *Adonai* (3.141592**65**358), the pronounceable component of the Tetragrammaton that is found exactly **92** times in the Pentateuch (3.1415**92**65358).

～

Just in case we harbor any lingering doubts about these admittedly rather otherworldly connections, let's consider that there are exactly 358 phrases in the Pentateuch (Torah) that have the value 314. Can this be coincidence? Maybe, but man thirty-four hundred

---

[4]Most superstring theories call for ten dimensions, but the bosonic string theory requires twenty-six dimensions.

years ago didn't know anything about pi. It wasn't even until 360 years ago that Sir Isaac Newton, a student of the sages' writings and of the second-century *Zohar,* calculated pi to the tenth digit, including 358.

~

SHADDAI

There's yet another link between pi, *Shaddai,* and the number **42**. According to the sages, the three letters in *Shaddai* (שדי), or **314**, can be broken into their component parts, with the *shin* (ש) becoming three *vavs* (ו, ו, ו), and the *dalet* (ד) becoming a *dalet* and its right facing lip a *yud* (ד, י), which means the three letters total to **42**. Moreover, the fourth root of **314** (*Shaddai,* Metatron, and pi) is also **4.20** . . .

~

It's obvious that the Torah was not constructed randomly, nor is it some simple historical novel, but that doesn't mean that God wrote it, either. It's hard to imagine who could, or who could have known about pi to thirteen digits or about square roots, or who could have kept track of all those letters, words, names, verses, phrases, rows, columns, and so on to have been able to integrate them so precisely into such a profound document. If someone could have done it, why did they design it to revolve around the Names of God?

~

NUMBERS

Numbers in both ancient *gematria* and modern number theory can be taken as a sum total of the individual letters or the numbers that represent them. Or, when we use the highly revelatory small *gematria,* the letters/numbers can be taken as a string of the individual digits in those numbers. And thus the first verse,

בראשית ברא אלהים את :השמים ואת הארץ
והארץ היתה תהו וב ←

can be translated as we did earlier into 913, 203, and so forth, or into a string of numbers. Using the small *gemaтria*$_{(0)}$ cipher to quantify the first verse, we get the numeric string 22130422113 50414534046145129651295045456662, but if we add up the square roots of each of these first 28 of the numbers corresponding to the exact first verse itself we get, astonishingly, **42.42**49**13**, and if we add up the square roots of the small *gematria*$_{(1)}$ for each of these entire **42** numbers, we get **73**. . . . once again. Don't let the use of the different ciphers for different equations fool you; it only adds deeper levels of complexity to the document. It's far easier to design and encrypt a document to spell out codes using a single cipher than to make each letter and word work triple time and spell out the same redundant message with differing encryption systems.

∼

So not only do the first **42** letters of the Bible spell out a co-herent and deep-meaning sentence, but they numerically form a simple equation that equates to pi, the primordial constant. More-over, their individual square roots sum to 73, the same integer that the sum of their full values also equaled. And, of course, 73 trans-lates to *Chochma*/wisdom. This is only the tip of the iceberg.

We said at the outset of the book that the total 390,625 words, letters, and verses of the Torah are, amazingly, equal to 5^8, or $5 \times 5 \times 5 \times 5 \times 5 \times 5 \times 5 \times 5$, but that it would be more astonish-ing if they *had* to equal that number. Now we can comprehend why, because the cube root of the 5^8 major Pentateuch elements, or $\sqrt[3]{(390625)} = 73.100 \ldots$, the same as the Creation Equation we're about to see built into the Bible's first verse, showing once again that the entire design of the Torah is reflected in its first **42** letters. Can we ask for a better indication of how important these first **42** letters are to us?

❧

THE ARK OF THE COVENANT

A further indication that the sum of the 3 major elements of the Torah being 5^8, or **390625**, was no fluke is shown by the fact that the inverse of the "Ark of the Covenant (256)" or $1/256 = 1/2^8 = .00390625 = 5^8/10^8$. Therefore, the Torah is the inverse of the Ark which hosts it. Moreover, the difference in the sums of the first 28 letters of the Torah and of the first 28 letters of the Genesis Prayer is the same as the "Ark of the Covenant": $2701 - 2445 = $ **256**.

❧

HOW FITTING IS IT THAT 42 + 31 (*EL*) = 73?

Further numerical and structural evidence that the Torah was designed around the level of *Chochma*/wisdom and thus around the number 73 is found in the total of its nonwritten elements. The sum of the 80 parchment pages, 248 columns, 10,400 rows, and 2 dowels = 10,730. Moreover, the numerical value for Moses (משה) and also for God (*Hashem*, השם), 345, is found 730 times, while the fifth word in the Bible, "the heavens," is repeated 73 times. As for the Genesis Prayer, the square root of the sum of the Torah occurrences of all **42** of its letters, meaning the square root of the amount of *alefs* and *bets* and so on as they occur in the Torah, is also 730.

❧

The Torah is nothing if not redundant. The most powerful connection of all to pi is found when we take the Genesis Prayer as a string of **42** letters—just like we did with the first **42** letters of Genesis—and convert them into numbers through small *gematria*$_{(0)}$:

← אבגיתצקרעשטן נגדיכ שבטרצתגחקבטנעיגלפזקשקוצית

123049027395534023292943802957033870306904

When we divide the number 9, as in the 9 numbers in pi lead-ing up to 358, the Messiah, or as in the nineth level/dimension, *Chochma,* by this Genesis Prayer string, we get:

9/.1230490273955340232929438029570338703069
04 = **73.1415777**
*Astonishingly,***73.1415777** *is off from true pi by only*
.000475 percent.

TRUE PI

It's even closer to true pi by an entire order of magnitude if we di-vide by only the Genesis Prayer's powerful first line: 9/.123049 =
73.141593 . . . off from true pi by **.000042** percent

In Appendix Five we provide more than sixty equations link-ing the Genesis Prayer to the Bible's first verse and both of them to the Names of God, the Messiah, pi, *Chochma,* and creation. There's even one linking it to phi, the primordial constant that con-trols spiraling growth in the universe. The Torah unfolded for me as a mathematical road map into the workings of the universe, or at least of how the Genesis Prayer interacts with it. None of it, though, is more important than the actual reciting of the prayer it-self. That's where the real miracles are.

NO BEGINNING AND NO END

It's important to note that the Israelites weren't alone at Mt. Sinai. According to the Pentateuch and all the sages there were 70 nations who received the Pentateuch (Torah), and what is 73.141592654, but 70 + pi (3.14159265 . . .). And of course, 28 + 42 = 70, so what could be more obvious? Moreover, 70 is the value for the word *sod,* secret.

We're beginning to grasp the full power and meaning of the Genesis Prayer and the Pentateuch's first verse. It appears the Genesis Prayer is the key to reunifying the 70 nations of the world, bringing our world back to that primordial state of pure consciousness that existed before the sin of Adam, helping to connect all 70 nations to the innumerable gifts of the Pentateuch (Torah) at the seed level. The sages tell us there are 70 Names of God, 70 Faces of God, and 70 angels hosting the Throne of God; and 70 faces (valid interpretations) of the Torah; and the 10 commandments, connecting to the 10 dimensions (*sefirot*), were given at the start of the 70th chapter in the Torah, so we can get an even better picture of the power the Genesis Prayer connects us to.

~

ADAM

The Bible tells us Adam lived 930 years, and the sages tell us that his 930 can be reunified with the 70 Nations to reunite us with *Keter*, the crowning dimension of God, in that $930 + 70 = 1,000$. The scientists show us another version of this in that the sum of the logarithms of the digits 1 through $70 = 100.0 \ldots$

~

Seventy is also a connection to the 70 elders who left Canaan and entered the exile into Egypt, also the 70 elders chosen by Moses, and according to the sages, the 70 levels of comprehension concealed within the Pentateuch (Torah). 70 is also the numerical value of "Adam and Eve," and of *Gog and Magog*, Armageddon, as in the apocalypse, which was first described by Enoch 5,000 years ago. From Adam to Armageddon, 70 is associated with "the beginning and the end," which may be why it's so intimately linked to pi and the Genesis Prayer through the simple Creation Equation:

$$9/\text{Genesis Prayer} = (70 + \text{pi})$$

The essence of pi is that it converts a line, which has a definitive beginning and end, and bends it into a circle, in which there is no beginning and no end, and in which there is only unity and wholeness. One of the deepest secrets of the sages was that our world is a line and that the "World to Come" is a circle; now we can see that the link to those two worlds and the reunification of the 70 nations is the Bible's first verse and the Genesis Prayer, and our interaction with them. Most of us are familiar with the term "the alpha and the omega," meaning "The beginning and end, the Almighty," and also "no beginning and no end," but that phrase is just Greek for the original term, the *Alef* and the *Tav,* as in the first and last letters of the Genesis Prayer.

~

NINE

The longest repetitive digit in pi is 9 digits long, for all the trillions of digits that we've been able to calculate so far, and there are exactly 9 Names for God used in the entire Pentateuch (Torah). And the longest repetitive sequential number in Pi is 242424242, which is not only 9 digits long but is found at digit #242424.

~

The very first word of the Bible was encoded with the double meaning of "the beginning and the end." That word, *beresheit,* which means "in the beginning," has the numerical value 913. The word value 913 reoccurs 6 times in the Torah; in other words, there are 6 words in the Torah whose letters total to a value of 913. The last four of those words translate to "its ends," conveying once again the concept of time without end, circle, and the unity of no beginning and no end.

The real clue is provided in the Name Almighty. As we've seen, "the alpha and omega" is the embodiment of the Genesis

Prayer, which begins and ends with *Alef* (א) and *Tav* (ת), and whose seventh line encompasses the first and last words of the Torah, as well as definitive allusions to the names of all five books together and to the entire text as a whole. Moreover, we've seen that the Name Almighty has a value of 314, making it synonymous with pi, which we've also seen to be integrally related to the Genesis Prayer and to its source, the Bible's first verse. Now, knowing that the function of pi is to take finite objects and convert them into endless ones (lines to circles, and so on), we can see why the sages called the Genesis Prayer "the **42**-letter Name of God"; it truly is the alpha and omega, our connection to the endless.

There is, though, one stronger connection yet. The 73, as in the Creation Equation 9/Genesis Prayer = 73.14159265 . . . , is represented in Hebrew/Aramaic as עג, which is also the world *ag*, meaning "to circle" or "to draw a circle." The only way to do that physically is to use pi. The only way to do it spiritually is to use the Genesis Prayer, drawing a circle of protection, unity, and understanding.

THE DESTRUCTION OF THE TEMPLES

It's not only the numbers and their associated energies and meanings that are programmed into the Pentateuch, but some of our history as well. Remember, there are 70 layers of meaning hidden in the Bible's first verse, and in one of them we can find that the value for the word *seventy (shivim)* is **422**, an integral part of the numerical sequence generated by the Torah's first verse:

בראשית ברא אלהים את השמים ואת הארץ:
והארץ היתה תהו וב = ←

221304**422**11350414534046145129651295045456662

It's right up front, the link between "in the beginning" and "create."

꜄

THE VAST COUNTENANCE OF GOD

It's not only right there "in the beginning," but when we divide the sequence into its 7 first words and add them, we get a total value of **294220**. That's what math tells us. The sages tell us the number 422 is also the value for *Arik Anpin,* the Vast Countenance of God, which the second-century *Zohar* tells us is at the highest level, the crowning level of *keter,* **1,000**, which may explain spiritually why the sum of all the logarithms of the integers from 1 to **70** is **100.0** . . .

꜄

Now, knowing all that 70 and 422 are associated with, it's not ironic that the Second Temple was destroyed for lack of unity in 70 C.E., and the First Temple in 422 B.C.E., or that the First Temple was destroyed in the Hebrew year 3338, which can be easily derived by dividing the number of letters in the Pentateuch (Torah) by the value of its first word, "in the beginning": 304805/913 = 333.85

Couple this with what we discussed in an earlier box of how the number of words in the first verse generates an equation equaling 5913 and that 5/9/1313 B.C.E. was the date the Israelites arrived at Mt. Sinai, and we can see why it's said that Enoch knew all. It had all been written and encoded. All he had to know was where to look. I'm afraid we're not Enoch, and it's not possible for us to know all. With a few pointers from the sages we're simply stabbing in the dark, which is why we need to listen to the little that we do know. We know that the Genesis Prayer can eventually take us to the highest levels—*Chochma* as individuals, and *Keter* as a unified society. We know that there's so much more out there than meets our eyes, so much more than we'll ever comprehend, but we also know that we don't have to understand all—the Genesis Prayer can make all the necessary connections for us. We know that we need help, lots of it, and that the universe wants to give it to us. We know that the Genesis Prayer is our cosmic nexus to the universe.

THE MESSIAH CONSCIOUSNESS

We can go on and on, analyzing the numbers and equations for spiritual significance, but we're just diluting all the miraculous benefits of the Genesis Prayer. Far more important for us is to start using the Genesis Prayer to bring all these miracles and wonders into our lives. It's time we reconnect to the universe, to creation, and use the Genesis Prayer to play *our* part in bringing unity and human dignity to the whole world, changing its consciousness by changing our own.

The other primordial mathematical constant that came into being at the moment of creation is phi (1.61803399 . . .). Recently made famous by Dan Brown's *The Da Vinci Code,* the Greeks called it the golden mean because it governs all the spiraling growth in the universe, from the petals on a flower and the branches of a tree to our DNA and the arms of the Milky Way. And like pi, it, too, also links inextricably to the Bible and the Genesis Prayer.

⤳

PHI, THE MESSIAH, AND THE BIBLE

Because the Torah's five structural elements—the words, letters, verses, columns, and the rows—equal 401273, and because the core Torah number 248 is so representative of the Torah, including being the sum of the names of its five books (2480), the equation 401273/phi (1.61803399) = 248000 is incredibly telling and beautiful. It also links us to both the Torah and the Genesis Prayer's fourth and seventh lines. There is so much more going on in this simple equation [401273/Phi (1.61803399) = 248000], though, such as 401 being the value of the Bible's fourth and also most numerous word value and 127 being the total possible combinations of the 7 words of the Bible's first verse, and 73 being so integral to that verse and the Genesis Prayer, and so on. Nevertheless, phi's integration into the Torah is even more profound because 358 is the numerical value for the Messiah and because Phi can be multiplied by the numeric string generated by the Bible's first verse to give us 3.580777 . . . as in Phi (1.61803398 . . .) × 221304221135041453404614512965129504545662 = 358.0777 . . . It's yet another improbable example of a constant that existed before the dawn of time tied to a document created before the existence of calculators or even long division.

❧

Just in case we think that changing our consciousness to the Messiah consciousness wasn't the point of the Bible and the Genesis Prayer, we can multiply the first 28 letters of Genesis by the first 28 letters of the Genesis Prayer and sum them up to get 358, the Messiah. With each one of those letters being a fountain and gateway to power, knowledge, and miracles, think what that multiple energy can do for you! Think of the power over life you'll have by connecting to it! Think of the changes you can make in the world!

19

It's Our Time

HOW DO WE KNOW THAT THE TIME IS RIGHT FOR US TO receive all this wonderful knowledge and wisdom that's hidden in the Pentateuch (Torah) and the Genesis Prayer?

The sages have told us so.

But wouldn't God have given us a signal?

Maybe He has. Of course, it's all speculation, and unlike the equations above, where if the result equates to pi, it's pretty obvious it's a purposeful design, in these equations the results depend on our level of skepticism. After all, results such as 2,000 and 5,760 can be just numbers or they could indeed be the year 2000 C.E. and its Hebrew equivalent, 5760. It's for this reason that we must limit ourselves to the spiritually significant Biblical numbers and to the clues provided by the sages, and even then, admittedly, it's just a supposition.

The 80,000 idealized, or realized, or completed words of the Pentateuch (Torah) can be divided by the one number in the Bible that symbolized the coming of age and spiritual readiness, 40 years, as the age that most of the Patriarchs, leaders, kings, prophets, and sages had to attain before being considered ready, to give us the simple equation 80,000/40 = 2000, as in the year 2000 C.E. We can also get the year 2000 C.E. by multiplying the 50 chapters in the Pentateuch's first Book by the 40 chapters in the second: $50 \times 40 = 2000$, which may seem random, except that the sages insist that 50 represents both the 50 Gates of Enlightenment (*Binah*) and of Judgment (*Gevurah*) and thus the upper and lower limit of man's consciousness. Thus it's explained that this equation really means the coming of a new age and the completion of a prior one.

The sages referred to our generation as the "generation of knowledge," and though they often worked hard to make it happen faster, they calculated that we'd be the ones receiving the Messiah, and thus the year 2000 (5760) can be thought of as a juncture or turning point, one that begins a generation destined to utilize the Genesis Prayer and to attain the Messiah consciousness—the consciousness that can bring about the Messiah.

THE FINAL LETTER

Another connection to the year 2000 is found by examining the Pentateuch's midpoint in letters, the place where the 304805 letters are split in half. Right at this junction in Leviticus 8:28, the number of *tavs* (ת), the alphabet's and the Genesis Prayer's *final* letter, are also split evenly, with 8955 on either side, and when we multiply the 8955 *tavs* by their value, 400, we get 3582000, or the Messiah (358) and 2000. Moreover, the value for the word *tav* is 406, which is the sum of the integers 1 through 28.

THE LONGEST WORD

The longest word (ובמשארותיך) in the Pentateuch (Torah) has 10 letters and is found once, at what the sages tell us is a very significant location within the 10 plagues. Without even knowing any of the sages' ancient technology, we can see that its location at Exodus 7:28 connects us to the Bible's first verse's 7 words and 28 letters and that it starts off with the Hebrew shorthand (במש) for the 42-letter Name. Interestingly, there are 4240 letter *nuns* in the Torah up to this word, with 424 being the value for the Messiah, *Mashiach Ben David,* and *nun,* with a value of 50, is representative of the fiftieth and final gate (negative and positive). At the time of the 10 plagues it was negative. Moreover, until this verse there are exactly 7,000 *mems* and 4,000 *shins* in the Torah, but even more telling is that the sum of all the letter values in the Torah through this unique 10-letter word is **5760**450, as in the year 5760 (2000 C.E.).

Now there are many, many proofs of a divine calendar, so we won't list them here; nevertheless, a perfect example of the Bible's signal to us is found in the 613 precepts spelled out in the Pentateuch (Torah). Of them, 365 are restrictive ones (don't do this, don't do that) and 248 are proactive ones, leading us to the ancient *gematria* equation: $3 \times 6 \times 5 \times 2 \times 4 \times 8 = 5760$, the Hebrew Calendar equivalent of the year 2000 C.E. And though it's not proof that this equation, derived from the precepts at the heart of the Pentateuch (Torah) and subsequently of Judaism, refers to the year 5760, the sages point to another revelatory *gematria* equation, $3 + 6 + 5 + 2 + 4 + 8 = 28$, to illustrate just how significant these results are meant to be, for 28 is the ubiquitous key number upon which the entire Torah revolves.

The 365 prohibitive and 248 proactive precepts, or spiritual guideposts, reveal much more than just the date of the recent millennium. We've already highlighted many other things that 248 represents, including Abraham and Raziel, but what of 365? Obviously, there are 365 days in the year, but what else?

THE SIDEREAL YEAR

There are 365 days in the year, but more specifically there are exactly 365.256 days in the more spiritual sidereal year, the measure of the Earth's revolution against the background of the cosmos and constellations. And, of course, 256 is another of our core Pentateuch numbers, representing the Ark of the Covenant, "Aaron," and 2^8, but when we divide the days in the sidereal year by 4, symbolizing the Tetragrammaton, we get $365.256/4 = 91.314$, connecting Genesis (913) once again with pi (314) and thus creation.

When we do the simple division of our Genesis Prayer/pi link by 2(000), or $73.14157771495/2(000) = 36.5708 \ldots$, we get 365 coupled with 5708, the year Israel became a nation again—Israel, the last word in the Pentateuch and the last word numerically spelled out in the **42** letters of the Genesis Prayer.

777

Further clues to the depth of this simple equation are provided by the 777 in 73.14157**771**495, which is the same numerical value as the three nouns—God, Heaven, and Earth—in Genesis's first verse, and also by the 1495 in 73.141577**1495**, which is the sum of all 22 numerical values of the Hebrew/Aramaic alphabet, from which all our *gematria* are derived. (Just like the sages told us: Not a digit or a letter wasted.)

ENOCH, THE CHANNEL

And even more simple than $73.14157771495/2 = 36.5708$ is $73/2(000) = 36.5$, with 73 being the value most representative of the first verse, creation, and *Chochma*/wisdom. But the Torah is infinitely revealing, and 365 is not only the number of days in the year, but the number of years Enoch lived, which the Bible describes as 300 and 65. We know that 300 is the *atbash* value for the Tetragrammaton[5], while 65 is the value for *Adonai,* so it's pretty clear that the Bible wanted us to be sure that Enoch, the seventh in the line of Adam, was someone special, someone connected to God. And the sages tell us that the physical union of the Tetragrammaton with *Adonai* creates an open channel to God, a window between the upper and lower worlds, if you will. And through the Genesis Prayer, Enoch is that channel for us. According to the Bible, he never died but was taken away, and according to all the sages, he became an angel, the archangel Metatron, whose value is 314. Enoch's name reveals even more, because its numerical value is 84 *(yeda),* knowledge. It's also the sum of all the meditation elements of the Genesis Prayer all at once: the **42** letters, the 21 pairs, the 14 triplets, and the 7 lines.

Regardless, thanks to the Dead Sea Scrolls, we know that the *Books of Enoch* predated the time of Christ by at least three hundred years, and since they contain true verifiable prophesies that extended past the destruction of the Second Temple in 70 C.E., it's not inconceivable that his prophetic texts stretched back another thirty-eight hundred years to when the Bible and the sages tell us they did. What's important to us today about his prophecies is that many of the apostles used them in their writings, with over one hundred quotes or citations from them used in the New Testament. The *Books* themselves were part of the Bible until 325 C.E., when they and many other books were removed from most Bibles for various reasons. Moreover, it is common knowledge that the

[5] The Tetragrammaton (יהו׳ה) in *atbash* is מצפ׳צ, with a value of 300, which is also the value for the spelled-out form of *Elohim.*

Books of Enoch were widely read in the first century. A cursory reading of them makes plain that Luke and Matthew both were trying to line up Jesus's genealogy with the predictions in Enoch's books. Luke added four additional generations not listed in the Bible in order to place Jesus as the 77th generation after Adam, which sounds like a pretty prophetic number, but once the generations are properly set and King David becomes the 33rd generation in the lineage of Adam, Jesus moves up to the 73rd generation, the 40th generation after David, and as we've discussed 40 is the coming-of-age number for most of the key biblical events, but even more important, 73 is the primordial number connecting to creation, God, the Genesis Prayer, and Enoch.

Now, this doesn't mean anything other than a very prophetic birth, and regardless of anyone's religious beliefs, we already know that, because it heralded a paradigm shift in the makeup of the entire world. Of the *Books of Enoch,* though, there was one that was secretive, which only a few have studied. This was the book that originally went by the name the *Book of Raziel,* which the second-century *Zohar* tells us was changed to the *Book of Enoch* when it was given to him. As we described in the introduction, *The Book of Raziel* was given to Adam, then to Enoch, and on to his great-grandson, Noah. From there, who had it and who didn't is not known, other than that Abraham, Moses, and Solomon had it for sure and many, many sages quoted from it. From fragments found in the Dead Sea Scrolls we know the Essenes had it, too, so it's no surprise that many of the meditations feel familiar to us today.

Now it's time we put it all together—the letters, the meditations, and the consciousness. We're the generation of Knowledge, and it's time we live up to that moniker and use that knowledge to connect.

As for those 248 proactive and 365 restrictive precepts, how odd is it that 248 is the numerical value of the Archangel Raziel and 365 are the years of the life of Enoch, before he became the Archangel Metatron, whose numerical value is 314? Is it any wonder that the Genesis Prayer is coming out now? Is it just another coincidence that $3 \times 6 \times 5 \times 2 \times 4 \times 8 = 5760$, the Hebrew Calendar equivalent of the year 2000 C.E., or that Raziel-Enoch-Metatron is our connection to the Genesis Prayer and Creation and that it's only coming to light now?

Whether you're dazzled by the math or dizzied by it, the Genesis Prayer has been there waiting for you all your life. It's been there for all of us. The sages of blessed memory knew where to look for it and became prophets, healers, and tremendous miracle-makers. The whole universe opened up for them, all the blessings and wonders beyond our imagination. Now, it's here for us.

It's been a process that's taken us nearly six thousand years. Each one did his part, made his sacrifices, revealed a little, and kept a lot more concealed. Many windows of opportunity have opened and closed. Thanks to all those that came before us, the windows are open again.

The blessings are here for us now. The miracles are here for us now.

All we have to do is try.

We've been given a gift. Don't look it in the mouth.

Don't waste this opportunity. The door swings both ways.

Life isn't easy, but it could be. It could be a lot easier.

It could be a lot better for all of us, and if we all do our part it will be.

That part we need to play can take only five minutes a day.

Just by taking five minutes out of our daily stress and chaos to surround ourselves with the coddled warmth of the Creator and to wrap ourselves in the brightness of His Light, we can make each day better than the last. In no time at all, nothing in our lives will be the same. Suddenly people will be on time, our work will be well received, and smiles will be on the faces of everyone we deal with. Life will smile. So will the universe. So will you.

If you still feel after all this that it's some hocus-pocus with numbers and you can't relate to numbers, just try the Genesis Prayer for yourself. What do you have to lose? You might just find your soul mate. You might just find fulfillment. You *will* get a miracle.

And after all those cold numbers, it's good to reacquaint our-selves with the simple and pure warmth that's been built into the **42** letters of the Genesis Prayer: the first pair of letters spells *Av* (אב), father, while the numerical value **42** itself is that of *Ima* (אמא), mother. The values of father (3) and mother (42) built into the Genesis Prayer sum to 45, the value of Adam. And that's how much we're loved—just as much as the Creator loved Adam.

APPENDIX ONE

The Genesis Prayer

THE PURE *ANA B'KO'ACK*

Read Transliteration from Right to Left

THE 42 WORDS

...amaic Letters						
...ergy of ...e Month	The 42 Letters (14 Triplets)	Left ← Column	Central ← Column	Right ← Column		
		תַּתִּיר 'צְרוּרָה	גְּדוּלַת יְמִינְֶךָ.	אָנָּא בככֹנֹי׳	*Chesed*	
...uarius צ ב ...pricorn ע ב	אבג יתצ	Tsrurah Tatir	Yeminechah Gedulat	B'ko'ack Ana	Line 1
		טַהֲרֵנוּ נוֹרָא:	עַמְּךָ שַׂגְּבֵנוּ.	קַבֵּל רִנַּת	*Gevurah*	
...es ק ג ...ittarius ג ס	קרע שטן	Norah Taharenu	Sagvenu Amechah	Rinat Kahbel	Line 2
		כְּבָבַת שָׁמְרֵם:	יְחוּדְךָ יוֹזוֹרְךָ.	נָא גִבּוֹר.	*Tiferet*	
...rpio ד ג ...es ד ה	נגד יכש	Shomrem Kevavat	Yichudechah Dorshay	Gibor Na	Line 3
		תָּמִיד גָּמְלֵם:	רַחֲמֵי צִדְקָתְךָ.	בָּרְכֵם טַהֲרֵם.	*Netzach*	
... כ ט	בטר צתג	Gomlem Tamid	Tsidkatechah Rackamay	Taharem Barckem	Line 4
		נַהֲל עֲדָתֶךָ:	בְּרוֹב טוּבְךָ.	נָּסִין קָדוֹשׁ	*Hod*	
...go ר י ...nini ד ז	יגל פזק	Adatechah Nahel	Tuvchah Berov	Kadosh Khasin	Line 5
		זוֹכְרֵי קְדוּשָׁתֶךָ:	לְעַמְּךָ פְּנֵה	יָחִיד גֵּאֶה	*Yesod*	
...ra פ ל ...rus פ ו	חקב טנע	Adatechah Zocrey	P'nay L'amcha	Geh'eh Yackid	Line 6
		תַּעֲלוּמוֹת: יוֹדֵעַ	צַעֲקָתֵנוּ. וּשְׁמַע	שַׁוְעָתֵנוּ קַבֵּל.	*Malkut*	
...cer ח ת	שקו צית	Ta'alumot Yode'ah	Tsa'akatenu Ushma	Kahbel Shavatenu	Line 7

(ברוך שם כבוד מלכותו לעולם ועד)

(Va'ed L'olam Malckutoh Kevod Shem Baruch) ← (whisper silently)

Gematria *Ciphers for the Hebrew/ Aramaic Alphabet*

Hebrew/ Aramaic	Standard *Gematria*	Small *Gematria*$_{(0)}$	*Atbash*	Ordinal Position	Spelled-Out Letters	
א	1	1	400	1	אלף	111
ב	2	2	300	2	בית	412
ג	3	3	200	3	גמל	73
ד	4	4	100	4	דלת	434
ה	5	5	90	5	הי	15
ו	6	6	80	6	ויו	22
ז	7	7	70	7	זין	67
ח	8	8	60	8	חית	418
ט	9	9	50	9	טית	419
י	10	0	40	10	יוד	20
כ	20	2	30	11	כף	100
ל	30	3	20	12	למד	74
מ	40	4	10	13	מם	80
נ	50	5	9	14	נון	106
ס	60	6	8	15	סמך	120
ע	70	7	7	16	עין	130
פ	80	8	6	17	פא	81
צ	90	9	5	18	צדי	104
ק	100	0	4	19	קוף	186
ר	200	2	3	20	ריש	510
ש	300	3	2	21	שין	360
ת	400	4	1	22	תו	406

A Powerful Supplementary Meditation for Healing

THIS POWERFUL VISUAL MEDITATION FOR HEALING THAT goes hand in hand with the Genesis Prayer was revealed to us by one of the most knowledgeable sages of all time, the Ari Hakodesh, in his book the *Gates of the Holy Spirit*. He originally called it *Tikune HaNeshamah*, but it's more commonly known as the *Tikune HaNefesh*, and as you can see in the accompanying chart it consists of various vowel permutations of the Tetragrammaton (יהוה) aligned with specific parts of the body according to the different *sefirot* (dimensions) they draw upon. Both of the names of this meditation translate to "The Soul Corrective"; in other words, the meditation is a spiritual realignment of our soul. To the Hindus it's a cleansing of our chakras, and to the Chinese, it's painless acupuncture, a removal of the blockages in our *ch'i*, or life force, energy paths.

It may seem a little foreign to us unless we've been exposed to Eastern spirituality practices, but it's an extremely potent way to draw healing energies into our lives. Each area of the body has a different and very distinct energy level, and by properly energizing it on the spiritual level, we can correct flaws and energy deficits on the physical plane. We can think of those different Tetragrammaton permutations as tuning forks, each set to a different frequency.

By engaging them with our eyes and holding our right hand over the appropriate part of the body, we can realign our frequencies and those of the people for whom we're meditating. The vibrations will shake loose any negativity clinging there; they'll shake our weary DNA back into shape, knocking out free radicals and mutations caused by the environmental toxins we've been subjected to all our lives.

All we have to do is follow the sequences of the boxes. Using our right hand, the hand of sharing, as a guide, we want to channel the vision of the two letters of the month to the various parts of our bodies in sequence, projecting the letters like laser beams emanating from our hand. The trick is to meditate on other people and thus make ourselves a channel for the energy to flow through us. We want to think of people we know who need healing in general or especially in a specific area of the body, and if we're fortunate enough not to know of anyone, we can meditate on the sick people in the hospitals and so on. For people who have depression or psychiatric disorders we can concentrate on the first three boxes corresponding to the head.

The sages used to meditate on people by actually visualizing them and merging the person's body with their own in order to enhance the healing, and by thinking of the person's name and their mother's name; if the mother's name wasn't known, they'd replace it with the name Sarah, the Matriarch.

As you go through the boxes, be sure to make eye contact with the Tetragrammaton schematics, but don't try to pronounce them; the eyes are the windows to the soul and will download them directly to our DNA, correcting any flaw created by our prior negative actions.

Once you've lifted off that negativity, picture it disappearing and dissipating into the atmosphere. It's always good to do the *Tikune HaNefesh,* but I can't make any promises about its efficacy because it all depends on your certainty. Even your doctor will tell you that. Those patients who are given a diagnosis and a cure by their doctors, even if it's through a fake diagnosis and a placebo, will get better, and those that don't, even if their doctor is sincere and earnest, won't, at least not nearly as quickly as those who were encouraged. Medicine in the twenty-first century is as it was two thousand years ago; it's more mind over matter than material. It just costs more. The meditations in the *Tikune HaNefesh* go beyond the mind to the soul and thus can work on people who don't know they're being prayed for. That's why it worked for Martha (*Bli ayn hara*), and that's why Columbia University was able to prove that women halfway around the world can get pregnant more easily with the spiritual help of pure strangers.

Many of the meditations delineated by the Ari came about through his enlightened explanations of the highly encrypted second-century *Zohar,* itself a series of explanations and revelations about the encryptions of the Pentateuch (Torah), and as odd as it seems, the *Zohar* goes into detail describing such things as cholesterol and internal workings of the liver and gall bladder and how the **42** letters of the Genesis Prayer align with the **42** joints in our bodies, and all sorts of medical wisdom only recently discovered by modern medicine. So when the *Zohar* and the Ari tell us that anger is the seed of most disease and that when we get to the meditations for the nostrils we should exhale our anger like thick smoke, we should give them the benefit of the doubt; after all, it's exactly what today's doctors are telling us about stress, and what is stress but a form of anger?

So if you're feeling under the weather, go to your doctor, but also do the *Tikune HaNefesh* to give him a helping hand. It just might help him make that quick diagnosis and come up with a relatively painless cure. Remember, colds are often just cleansing—the body discharging its negativity from all its many levels, psychological emotional, physical, and spiritual.

Once done, go on to the next line of the Genesis Prayer. We only make one *Tikune HaNefesh* healing connection per Genesis Prayer, and it'll be at the same line all month, as per the charts in Appendix One and in Part V. It'll add from one to three minutes to the total meditation time, depending on how earnestly you're meditating for someone and how many different people you're meditating on. But even if you have no one you need to meditate for and even if you feel you're in great health, it's worthwhile making the healing connection because you never know. You never know what might be lurking inside or around the bend, and you never know when you'll need to tap into the goodwill you've created by meditating for others.

If you're trying to get pregnant, or know someone who is, you should meditate on line 16 and extend your meditation to everyone you know who is trying and everyone anywhere who's trying as well. That goes double for anyone who *is* pregnant, and if you are, you can do the *Tikune HaNefesh* healing meditation for the baby in your womb. It's a spiritual insurance policy.

TIKUNE HANEFESH
HEALING MEDITATION

Skull
(Keter)
יְהֹוָה   1

Left Brain
(Binah)
יְהֹוָה   3

Right Brain
(Chochma)
יַהֲוָה   2

Left Eye 5
יהוה   יהוה
יהוה
יהוה   יהוה

Nose

Right Eye 4
יהוה   יהוה
יהוה
יהוה   יהוה

Left Ear 7
יוד די ואו הה

יוד הי ואו הי

יוד הי ואו הי

Right Ear 6
יוד הי ואו הה

9   8

10

Mouth
יוד די ואו די (אלהיד)
אהה״ע גיב״ק דטלנ״ת זסשר״ץ בומ״ף

Left Arm
(Gevurah)
יְהֹוָה
12

Body
(Tiferet)
יְהֹוָה
13

Right Arm
(Chesed)
יְהֹוָה
11

Left Leg
(Hod)
יְהֹוָה
15

Reproductive Organs
(Yesod)
יודהווהו
16

Right Leg
(Netzach)
יְהֹוָה
14

Feet
(Malckut)
יְהֹוָה
17

Supplemental Daily Support Meditation

THIS FINAL MEDITATION TAKES ABOUT TWENTY SECONDS. All you have to do is scan, or glance at, without trying to pronounce the names of the angels—quantum energy messengers—on the box that corresponds to the energy of the day, paying particular attention where indicated by the arrows. As you do, ask that these messengers carry your requests and bring you answers, and that they conduct and strengthen all your connections, helping you to be proactive all day long, protecting you and your family.

As the energy is particularly powerful on the Sabbath, there are separate pages for Friday night after sunset, Saturday morning, and Saturday afternoon just before sunset, the most powerful time of the week for healing.

And that's it, all there is to it. It takes some practice, sure, but with every miracle, you'll see how worthwhile it is. The full complete Genesis Prayer shouldn't take you more than five minutes a day, five minutes to fulfillment.

Now, for those who want to grasp with true awe the beauty and technology that went into the Bible and the Genesis Prayer, the next section is for you.

DAILY ANGEL SUPPORT CHART

SUNDAY

יַוֹד הֵי וָאו הֵי גוֹד הֵי וָאו הֵי

אל שדי יאולדפהדהייואורדהיי

אנא בכוז גדולת ימינך תתיר צרורה

אֶבְגִיתֵץ יֱהוֹהֱ יֱהוֹהֱ

סְמְקֻוֹרָהֱ גַבְרִיאֵל מֶעוֹאֵל לְמוֹאֵל

ר״ת סגול

MONDAY

גוֹד הֵי וָאו הֵי וָאן הֵי וָאו הֵי יוֹד הֵא וָאו הֵא

אל יהוה יאולדפהדהאאיאוורדהאא

קבל רנת עמך שגבנו טהרנו נורא

קְרַעְשָטָן יֱהוֹהֱ יֱהוֹהֱ

שְׁמֵעָאֵל בְּרְכִיאֵל אֲדָנִיאֵל

ר״ת שׁוא

TUESDAY

יוֹד הֵא וָאו הֵא יוֹד הֵב עַב הֵב

אל אדני יאולדפהההההוירדהההה

נא גבור דורשי יחודך כבבת שמרם

נַגְדְיכַש יֱהוֹהֱ יהוה

וּנִזיאֵל להדיאֵל מוּוֹנִזיאֵל

ר״ת וולם

WEDNESDAY

יוֹד הֵא וָאו הֵא יוֹד הֵב עַב הֵב

אל אדני יאולדפהההההויורדהההה

ברכם טהרם רחמי צדקתך תמיד גמלם

בַּמַרְצְתָג יֱהוֹהֱ יהוה

חזְקִיאֵל רהְטִיאֵל קְדַשִׁיאֵל

ר״ת וורק

THURSDAY

גוֹד הֵי וָאו הֵי יוֹד הֵי וָאן הֵי יוֹד הֵא וָאו הֵא

אל יהוה יאולדפהדהאאיאוורדהדהאא

חסין קדיש ברוב טובך נהל עדתך

נַקְבַּמַע יֱהוֹהֱ יֱהוֹהֱ

שְׁמֵוֹאֵל רָמִיאֵל קָנִיאֵל

ר״ת שרק

FRIDAY

גוֹד הֵי וָאו הֵי וָאו הֵי גוֹד הֵי וָאו הֵי

אל שדי יאולדפהדהייואורדהיי

יוזור גאה לעמך פנה זוכרי קדושתך

יֱגַלְפֵזָק יֱהוֹהֱ יהוווהו

שׁוֹמַשְׁוֹויאוֹלו רופאוֹלו קורושׁוֹויאוֹלו

ר״ת שרק

FRIDAY NIGHT

יוֹד הֵי וָאו הֵי

שַׁוְעָתֵנוּ קַבֵּל וּשְׁמַע צַעֲקָתֵנוּ יוֹדֵעַ תַּעֲלוּמוֹת

שֶׁקֳוְצִית יַהֲוֹךְ יַהֲוֹךְ יַהֲוֹךְ

שְׁמָעִיאֵל בְּרַכְיָאֵל אֲהַנְיָאֵל

ר״ת שׁוֹא

סְמַטֹוְרַד גַּוְרִיאֵל וְעַנָּאֵל לְמַוָּאֵל

ר״ת סֶגּוֹל

צוֹהֲרִיאֵל רַזוֹאֵל וְוּפִיאֵל

ר״ת צִירִי

SATURDAY AFTERNOON

יוֹד הֵא וָאוֹ הֵא יוֹד הֵא וָאוֹ הֵא

שַׁוְעָתֵנוּ קַבֵּל וּשְׁמַע צַעֲקָתֵנוּ יוֹדֵעַ תַּעֲלוּמוֹת

שֶׁקֳוְצִית יַהֲוֹךְ יַהֲוֹנָד יַהֲוֹךְ

שְׁמָעִיאֵל בְּרַכְיָאֵל אֲהַנְיָאֵל

ר״ת שׁוֹא

פֶּרַאֵל תַּלְמַיַאֵל (תוֹמִיַאֵל) וַסַדְרִיַאֵל

ר״ת פתוֹז

SATURDAY MORNING

יוֹד הֵי וָנָו הֵי יוֹד הֵי וָנָו הֵי

שַׁוְעָתֵנוּ קַבֵּל וּשְׁמַע צַעֲקָתֵנוּ יוֹדֵעַ תַּעֲלוּמוֹת

שֶׁקֳוְצִית יַהֲוֹךְ יַהֲוֹנָד יַהֲוֹךְ

שְׁמָעִיאֵל בְּרַכְיָאֵל אֲהַנְיָאֵל

ר״ת שׁוֹא

קֳדָמְיָאֵל מָלְכָיָאֵל צַוְרְיָאֵל

ר״ת קמץ

Summary of Equations Linking Genesis and the Genesis Prayer with Pi and Thus Creation

I LEAVE IT TO THE READER TO DECIDE WHAT THESE EQUA-tions mean. They exist without any mathematical manipulation or interpretation whether we want them to or not. They've existed since the issuing of the very first Torah, and whether we believe that was on Mt. Sinai or not is irrelevant because even the latest date for the reception of the Torah was at a time before man was capable of making most of these equations, let alone incorporating them into a coherent three-hundred-thousand-plus-letter document. What it all means for you, you'll have to figure that out for yourself; what it meant for me was that through the Genesis Prayer I could connect to a source far beyond my comprehension. Remember, we didn't concern ourselves in this book with an infinite amount of numbers with an infinite amount of possibilities with which to play; we narrowly limited our assessment of the Pentateuch (Torah) to its first **42** letters and to pi's first 13 digits, to the 5 main and fixed structural elements of the Torah, and to a few key core names and words.

- The first 7 words connect to the 28 letters that comprise them through the sum of the integers through 7, or $28 = \Sigma(1\text{--}7)$. Both 7 and 28 are Triangular Numbers, which form equilateral triangles when laid out line by line, and 28 is also one of the very few perfect numbers in that the sum of its positive divisors is equal to twice itself. 28 is also the sum of the Abundant Number 12 (spiritually representative of the 12 tribes and, according to Abraham, the 12 constellations). Abundant Numbers are such that the sum of its positive divisors is greater than twice itself, and coincidentally or not, 24.8 percent of all positive integers are Abundant Numbers.

- The first 7 words connect to the first word of the Torah, whose value is 913, and to the date for the Israelites arrival at Mt. Sinai (5/9/1313 BCE) and to the value 73 through $\Sigma(1!-7!) = 7 \times 6 \times 5 \times 4 \times 3 \times 2 \times 1 + 6 \times 5 \times 4 \times 3 \times 2 \times 1 + \cdots = 5913$, and also through $5913/73 = 3^4$.

- The first word in Genesis is connected to the fifth, because the value (395) of the 5th word (the heavens) is the 913th value in the 5 Books of Moses in order of prevalence.

- The first 28 letters of Genesis are connected to the number 73 through their sum: $2701 = \Sigma(1-73)$.

- The first 28 letters of Genesis are connected to pi through their linear construction and *gematria* values: $[28 \text{ (letters)}/7 \text{ (words)}] \times [P_{gematria} 28 \text{ letters})/P_{gematria} (7 \text{ Words})] = 3.141545078 \times 10^{-07}$.

- The first 28 letters of Genesis are connected to pi and the number **42** though the average of the seven words that comprise those 28 letters: 42031.428 when the seven words are taken utilizing the small *gematria*$_{(1)}$ cipher: (221314 221 13514 14 53414 614 5129).

- The first 28 letters of Genesis are connected to **42**, to the Messiah (424), to "in the beginning" (913), and to heaven (390), through the sum of square roots of their small *gematria*$_{(0)}$ values: 42.42491390.

- The first **42** letters of Genesis are connected to 73 through the square roots[6] of those 42 letters: 73. . . .

- The first **42** letters of the Genesis Prayer, which the sages have shown is convertible into Genesis' first **42** letters, are even deeper connected

---

[6] One other connection is found in that the first two letters of the Hebrew/Aramaic alphabets are *alef* (א) and *bet* (ב) as in the first two letters of the Genesis Prayer: there are 7 alefs (א) and 3 bets (ב), making 73, among the first **42** letters of Genesis, and corresponding to the 7 lower dimensions *(sefirot)* and 3 upper ones.

to both 73^7 and pi through the number 9, the level of *Chochma*, whose value is 73: $9/.1230490\ldots = 73.1415777$.

- The 390,625, or 5^8, major Pentateuch elements are connected to the Name of God, *El*, through their cube root: $\sqrt[3]{390,625} = 73.3100$
- The first 28 letters of Genesis are connected to the first 28 of the Genesis Prayer and to the 390625 major elements of the Pentateuch through the difference in their sums: $2701 - 2445 = 256$, the value of the Ark of the Covenant and also of the title of the fifth book, Deuteronomy (*Devarim*), with $1/256 = 1/2^8 = .00390625$.
- The 390,625 elements also connect to the number 28 and to the idealized 80,000 words of the Torah through the natural squares. The 390,625 elements divided by the sum of all the square roots of all the natural numbers through the twenty-eighth natural square, or 28^2, equals precisely 80,000/3. In other words, $390,625/\Sigma(\sqrt{1-28^2}) = 80,000/3$, or 26.66662, off by only .000155% from an impossibly perfect 26.66666 . . . There are also exactly 80 words in the Torah whose numerical value is 358, the Messiah, and the exact number of words in the Torah is $(80,000 - .03\%)$, while 26 represents the Tetragrammaton, and the word "Torah" itself is repeated 26 times in the Torah.
- According to the sages, the 390625, or 5^8, major elements of the Torah connect to *Binah* and going above limitations through the 8th power and to the 5 worlds (levels of consciousness), 5 levels of soul, and 5 core dimensions (*sefirot*)—*Keter, Chochma, Binah, Zeir Anpin, and Malckut*. It's also representative of going above our 5 senses.
- The Name of God, *El* (31), is the first 2 digits in pi.
- The Name of God, *El* (31), is also connected to pi through *El's* value's cube root: $\sqrt[3]{31} = 3.1413806523913\ldots$ It's off from true pi by only .000021200, and 212 is the numerical value of "the Light," which is 424 (the Messiah) $\times$ .5.

[7] Incredibly, the sum of the square roots of the **42** letters in the Genesis Prayer in small *gematria*$_{(0)}$ is 73.0, and in small *gematria*$_{(1)}$ is 80.0, not only a reference to the idealized 80,000 words, but 7.0 more than 73.0, yet another reference to the 70 nations, the 7 words in the 1st verse, the 7 lines of the Genesis Prayer, etc.

- The Name of God, *El*, is also connected to the first word in Genesis (913) through *El's* cube root, $\sqrt[3]{31} = 3.1413806523913 \ldots$

- The name of God, *Shaddai,* the Almighty, and also the value of the highest archangel, Metatron, starts off pi (3.14159265358 . . .), while 358, the value for *Mashiach,* the Messiah, at the 10th digit and the sum of the 6 digits in between, is 28.

- The Name *Shaddai* (שדי), the Almighty, is found 10 times in the Torah.

- Other Names of God numerically encoded within the first 10 digits of pi include 31, 41, 15, 26, and 65: 31 (*El*, אל) is the first two digits (3.**14**159265358); 41 numerically spells *Yah,* the Lord (יהוה יה), and it is the number of letters in the spelled-out highest name of God, *Ehyeh* (אהיה), (3.1**4159**265358); 15 numerically spells *Yah* (יה) (3.1**4159**265358); and then comes 26, the Tetragrammaton (יהוה) (3.14159**265**358), attached to 65, *Adonai* (3.14159**265**358), the pronounceable component of the Tetragrammaton that is found exactly 92 times in the Torah (3.14**159**265358).

- Pi is connected to the Name of God, *El*, through the 8th root of its first 12 digits reversed: $\sqrt[8]{(853562951413} = 31.0031$. These are the digits through 358, the numerical value of the Messiah.

- Pi is connected to the name of God, *El,* through the sum of pi's first 8 digits: 31.

- Pi is connected to the Genesis Prayer through the square root of the sum of the occurrences in the Pentateuch of the six letters of the prayer's first line (אבגיתצ): 314.5727260 . . .

- 9 is connected to **42** in the same way that the **42** letters of the Genesis Prayer were connected to 73 and pi: 9 divided by the numerical sequence formed by the first verse in *Genesis* gives us 42.245 . . . and 422 is the value of the word for 70.

- Phi connects to the Pentateuch through the sum of the Torah's five structural elements—words, letters, verses, columns, and rows—split into the phi proportion, gives us 401273/phi (1.61803399) = 248000.

- The previous equation further links phi to the Torah in multiple ways, four of which are that 24.8 is the square root of 616, the numerical value of the word Torah"; that the sum of the numerical value of the 5 names of the 5 books is 2,480, while the sum of the integers through 70 or $\Sigma(1–70)$ is 2,485; that there are 248 proactive precepts listed throughout the Torah; and that 248 is the numerical value for Abraham and for the Archangel Raziel, and the Gregorian calander was adjusted so that the year 248 Anna Diocletinal become the year 532 AnniDomini.

- 248 is not only the value for the Torah's fourth Book, Numbers *(Bamidbar),* but there are 1,024 (2^{10}) unique word values in the Torah, and the sum of the integers through 1024 is 524,800, while $1024 = 5 \times 248$.

- The sum of all the square roots of all **42** letters of the Genesis Prayer taken together letter for letter with the Bible's first **42** letters using *gematria Albam* is 424.805, and while 424 is the messiah, *Meshiach Ben David*; and 2,480 is the sum of the numerical value of the five names of the five books, etc., 304,805 is the exact number of letters in the Torah, and 4805 is the exact number of the letter *pe* (פ) in the Torah, whose value of each is 80; and 805 is the value for "the rainbow," God's first covenant with man.

- Moreover, the sum of all the square roots of all 28 letters of the Bible's first verse and of the first 28 corresponding letters of the Genesis Prayers taken together letter for letter using *gematria Albam* is 286.11110, giving us the ubiquitous 28 numerically representing power, and so on; 611, representing "Torah"; and 110 representing "miracle."

- The total numerical value for the entire Genesis Prayer is exactly 1,000 more than that of Genesis's first verse $(3,701 - 2,701 = 1,000)$.

- The sum of the logs of the digits 1 through $70 = 100.0 \dots$, connecting, as the sages tell us, to *Keter,* the crown, the ultimate, uppermost of the 10 dimensions, the one encompassing the purest light force, the one closest to God.

- When comparing the standard values of the 7 first words of Genesis with the 7 lines of the Genesis Prayer, we see that the difference between them is 1,000, but since some of the words are of higher value than their corresponding lines and some are lower, the sum of the absolute values of their differences is 2,480.

- Dividing the sum of the Genesis Prayer by the sum of Genesis's first verse gives us $3,701/2,701 = 1.3702\ldots$, and 137 is the value of the word "to receive" (*Kabbalah*) and also the value of the alpha or fine structure constant, $1/137.0359$, the measure of the strength of the electromagnetic force that governs how electrically charged particles such as electrons interact with light, photons. Moreover, according to the *Zohar*, 359 is the *gematria* value for the Aramaic word for the Messiah.

- The sum of the Genesis Prayer, 3,701, also connects to 73 and to the sum of Genesis's first verse, 2701, because $3,701 \times .73 = 2701.73$.

- But what makes this all the more intriguing is that the alpha constant is $(1/137) = .73.$, or more precisely, $.0072992701$, which compares with $1/3701 = .0002701$, with 2701 being the value of the first verse of Genesis.

- The creation equation yields $73.141577 - pi = 70.00000$, corresponding to the 70 nations that received the Torah on Mt. Sinai, and the 70 Elders and 70 forefathers who entered Egypt, 70 faces of the Torah, 70 Angels that guard the throne of God, and so on.

- The 506 Genesis Prayer triplet occurrences in the Torah connect to *unconditional love*, whose value is 506, and to pi, 73, and **42** through the equation $3701/506 = 7.3142\ldots$.

- 3,142 is the small *gematria*$_{(1)}$ value of the famous phrase that God said to Moses at the burning bush, "I AM that I AM." The cube root of 3,142 is $28.0\ldots$ Moreover, the phrase is found at Exodus 3:14, and the regular *Gematria* value of the two "I AMs" (אהיה) is **42**. And whether this is coincidence or not, it's hard to say, but there are 6 word values found 26 (the Tetragrammaton) times each in the Pentateuch, and $6 \times 26 = 156$, the value of Yosef, who corresponds to the 6th line of the Genesis Prayer, but the incredible part is that those 6 word values total 3,142.

- And 73 is the value for the word *gimmel,* the name of the 3rd letter in both the alphabet and the Genesis Prayer, as in $3^2 = 9$ and as in the 3-column system. $73 \times 3 = 219$ and there are exactly 2109 *gimmels* in the Torah. If this is all pure coincidence, why is $2 \times 1 \times 9 = 18$, with the sum of all the natural squares through 18 being 2109.

- The number **42** is connected to the 3-column system and to the Bible's first verse's total value through the following integer sum equation: $3 \times (\Sigma 1\text{–}42) - (\Sigma 1\text{–}73) = 2709 - 2701 = 8 = 2^3$, as in the 8 lines of the Genesis Prayer.

- Further evidence of the intentional design of this verse and indeed of the entire Torah is found in that the 4th and 2nd words of the Bible have a total of 2,628 occurrences in the Torah, and $2{,}628 = \Sigma(1\text{–}72)$, or the sum of the integers through 72, while the 4th, 2nd, and 5th, words occur a total of 2,701 or $\Sigma(1\text{–}73)$ times.

- Finally, 9 is not only representative of the level *Chochma,* but also the longest repetitive number in pi for the trillions of digits that have been calculated so far is 9 digits long; and 9 spaces separate the paragraphs in the Pentateuch. Moreover, there are exactly 9 Names for God used in the entire Pentateuch, and one of those Names, *Elo'ah* (אלוה) has the value **42.** Also, the word value of 9 is found 26 (Tetragrammaton) times in the Pentateuch, and the actual word for nine (תשע) is also found exactly 9 times, while there are 9 chronicles in Genesis and 9 *yuds* in the complete Tetragrammaton—the fully spelled version of its 4 aspects.

- Using their small *gematria*$_{(1)}$ values, both the first line of the Genesis Prayer and the first word of Genesis contain the number 314: the Bible begins with בראשית, 221314, as does the Genesis Prayer with אבגיתצ, 123149. Moreover, the first verse of the Genesis Prayer also includes the 9 from the creation equation: 9/(Genesis Prayer) = 73.141 . . .

- The 304,805 letters multiplied by the 79,975 words multiplied by the 5,845 verses of the Torah = 142,482,278,369,375, which breaks down to: 1424, meaning *Kadosh Kadoshim,* "Holy of Holies," the most central inner sanctum of the Holy Temple; 424, *Mashiach Ben David,* the Messiah; 248, Abraham, and so on; 22 Hebrew/Aramaic letters; 278, the *Gematria* and Ezra, who rebuilt the second Temple and by all accounts penned the exact same Torah as Moses, the one we read today; 36 Righteous souls, etc.; and 9,375, which is the numerical difference of the ultimate limit (ת or 400) and the number of words, letters, and verses in the Torah, or (400,000 − 390,625).

- The sum of the values of the 22 spelled-out letters of the Hebrew/ Aramaic alphabet is 4,248 as in the multiple of the 3 main Torah elements, 142,482,278,369,375. And the sum of the 7 square roots of the 7 lines of the Genesis Prayer when the **42** letters are spelled out is 248.503631, representing Abraham (248), etc.

- Incidentally, 390,625 is 5^8 and $400,000 = 5 \times 80,000$, while 9,375 is $(5^5 + 5^5 + 5^5)$, and since we know the importance of the 3-column system and that 5 represented to the sages the highest levels and the full inclusion of all the worlds and all the possible levels, we also know that none of this is coincidence. $5^8 = 5 \times 80,000 - (3 \times 5^5) = 5^4 \times 2^7 - (3 \times 5^5)$.

- 390,625 is also the result of multiplying the 22 Hebrew/Aramaic letters by the sum total of their value (1,775), when the five final values (280) are included, plus 5^3: $1,775 \times 22 \times 10 + 5^3 = 390,625$.

- $390,625\sqrt{(\sqrt{1} + \sqrt{2})} = 1,618,022$, off by only .000754% from an impossibly exact phi (1.618033). In other words, 390,625 divided by the sum of the square roots of the first two natural numbers = phi.

- Also most enlightening is that the sum of the logarithms of the 3 major components (79,975 words, 304,805 letters, and 5,845 verses) is 14.153760 . . . , which is very reminiscent of pi, 3.1415, and is evocative of the Hebrew calendar year 3760, or 0 C.E.

- The Genesis Prayer begins with אבגיתצ, 123,149, and when we permute the letters/numbers—which according to R. Eliezer (Ro'keack), the great teacher of "the Ramban,"/Nachmanides, is one of the 73 ways to understand and interpret the letters of the Torah—we get 1 913 42 in small *gematria*[1] and 0 913 42 in small *gematria*[0]. In either case, the multiple interpretations are similar and clear: In the 1st verse of Genesis (913) (or alternatively, "In the beginning"), there was the **42**-Letter Name of God.

- The 203000 from the product of the two triplets of the seventh line (ציח × שקו) connect's to pi, the Torah, and also with Moses through the equation 203,000/pi = 64616.9068 . . . , which breaks down to the **646** total times the name Moses is used in the Torah; and the **616** times Moses is mentioned without prefixes; and to the meaning of the value 616, which is "The Torah"; and to 906, which is the value of the sum of these 2 triplets (צִיץ + שֶׁקֶר). Moreover, 906 is also the sum of the standard *gematria* value and its complimentary *atbash* value of the Bible's first 3 letters combined (בְּרָא), which in standard *gematria* would simply be 203.

- *The Alpha and the Omega.* Just as the Genesis Prayer begins and ends with *alef* (א) and *tav* (ת), the original alpha and omega, the allusion is repeated through the *gematria* of the Genesis Prayer's final line. Through standard *gematria* the full value of this line (plus the *kolel, 7,* for the 7th line) is 913, the same as the Torah's first word (*beresheit*), "in the beginning," while through *gematria atbash* the last triplet of this same line has the value 541, numerically representing Israel, the Torah's last and final word. The sages tell us that the Torah's last verse cycles back to its first, closing the circle and leaving us with 5,845 total verses, rather than 5,846. These two verses are so integrated that the entire Hebrew calendar is derived from their combination, one example of which is that their combined number of words is 19, which corresponds to their greater 19-year cycle, and while the 7 words in the first verse correspond to their smaller 7-year cycle, the 12 words in the last verse correspond to their 12-month lunar cycle.

Index

About the Author

JEFFREY MEILIKEN, a mathematician with twenty years' experience analyzing the commonalities of ancient cultures, is a leading authority on the structural encryptions embedded in the artifacts of many of these cultures, including the Nazcas of Peru, the Egyptians, and the early Israelites. A student of spirituality for even longer, he frames this hidden knowledge within the context of each culture's esoteric wisdom. Having lived many years overseas, including eight years in South America, he currently lives in Manhattan with his wife and two young children. A corporate consultant on the use of influential numbers and the author of several books, he travels the country giving seminars on the Genesis Prayer and lecturing on ancient encrypted mathematics.